✳ ✳ ✳

"Those of us who are both Black and autistic have stories to tell, and the moment to share them is now. This is an important work that weaves together a tapestry of lived experiences that have historically remained obscured. For those who seek to deepen their understanding of Black autistic experiences and foster an environment of empathy and change, this book is a must-have for the bookshelf."
—**Morgan Harper Nichols,** autistic author and artist

"In *Autistic and Black*, Kala Allen Omeiza masterfully weaves together 20 poignant voices, creating an impressive tapestry charting diverse journeys with autism across global landscapes. A transformative exploration of identity, love, and advocacy, this book is a testament to resilience and the vibrant tapestry of the Black autistic experience."
—**Montreece Payton-Hardy,** accessibility and disability inclusion specialist, writer, and speaker, Disabled Babes Book Club member

"Kala's book *Autistic and Black* paints a diverse and enriching picture of lived experiences. I was transported across continents through the pages of the book and the lens of neurodivergence. The message of the book was thus conveyed so artistically, making it a must-read for any and everyone!"
—**Dr. Bolu Ikwunne,** Rhodes Scholar, University of Oxford, Department of Psychiatry

"It is always wonderful when people are allowed to tell their own story. Reading Kala's book felt like sitting with friends, who are invited—finally—to share their personal experiences of being autistic. *Autistic and Black* is a wonderful read."
—**Neurodiversity Society,** University of Oxford

✳ ✳ ✳

AUTISTIC AND BLACK

of related interest

Black, Brilliant and Dyslexic
Neurodivergent Heroes Tell their Stories
Edited by Marcia Brissett-Bailey
Foreword by Atif Choudhury
ISBN 978 1 83997 133 4
eISBN 978 1 83997 134 1

Autistic World Domination
How to Script Your Life
Jolene Stockman
ISBN 978 1 83997 444 1
eISBN 978 1 83997 445 8

Taking off the Mask
Practical Exercises to Help Understand and Minimise
the Effects of Autistic Camouflaging
Dr Hannah Belcher
Foreword by Will Mandy, PhD, DClinPsy
ISBN 978 1 78775 589 5
eISBN 978 1 78775 590 1

Autistic & Black

Our Experiences of Growth, Progress, and Empowerment

Kala Allen Omeiza

Jessica Kingsley Publishers
London and Philadelphia

First published in Great Britain in 2024 Jessica Kingsley Publishers
An imprint of John Murray Press

1

Copyright © Kala Allen Omeiza 2024

Some names of interviewees have been changed to protect
their identities.

Content warning: abuse, bullying, racism, suicide, trauma, violence

A CIP catalogue record for this title is available from the
British Library and the Library of Congress

ISBN 978 1 83997 620 9
eISBN 978 1 83997 621 6

Printed and bound in Great Britain by TJ Books Ltd

Jessica Kingsley Publishers' policy is to use papers that are
natural, renewable and recyclable products and made from wood
grown in sustainable forests. The logging and manufacturing
processes are expected to conform to the environmental
regulations of the country of origin.

Jessica Kingsley Publishers
Carmelite House
50 Victoria Embankment
London EC4Y 0DZ

www.jkp.com

John Murray Press
Part of Hodder & Stoughton Ltd
An Hachette Company

For my family and friends around the world. Stay blessed.

Contents

Introduction

Ujima

Black. Autistic. Enough.

I have to confess: my family never celebrated Kwanzaa. The relatively recent Black American holiday celebrates community, togetherness, unity, and culture. I deeply enjoyed learning about this tradition when I was in school. This celebration seemed empowering, and the noted connection to our African ancestry seemed emotional and fulfilling. I wondered why my family didn't celebrate. At first, I would have guessed that my military family simply moved around too often to commit to establishing a routine outside of our Christian holidays. I'm sure it was challenging to commit to reflect on our trials and triumphs, as is instructed in the third principle of Kwanzaa, Ujima. However, looking back on my childhood with adult lenses, I wonder if my family felt qualified. My family of six (two parents, three children, and one cat) rarely lived within five hours of our extended family, much less celebrated the holidays with them. Ujima, for example, means "Collective Work and Responsibility" in Swahili (Medearis, 1994). On the outside, with

Western community standards, we seemed to be lacking the true meaning behind Kwanzaa: **Community**.

I was diagnosed with autism spectrum disorder at 24 years old. For many years before, I admired the tenacity of my mom, and the extroversion of my dad. I often mentally noted words and phrases that my dad said in conversations with his lifelong friends, and attempted to repeat those phrases out of context with strangers. Of course, my attempts at saying "It's a catch-22" when a classmate asked me if we had a test next week, or "That's a home run right there" to onlookers at a track meet, did not appear to go over well. My family, however, never seemed to be concerned about my feelings of being an outsider. To them, I was a part of the family like they were. Sure, we didn't have several cousins or other extended family members routinely around, but we really did practice the spirit of Kwanzaa every day of our lives. The unique backgrounds of my parents coupled with the diverse personalities of my siblings and myself made one strong unit that stayed tight as we went from eating on tatami mats to tables, traveling in moving vans to military planes, and from celebrating graduations to weddings. My family was not only a unit but a: **Community?**

As I entered adulthood, that word became more important to me. Naturally, I longed to befriend more Black people, and to maybe have a "friends-Kwanzaa" in the same way people celebrate "Friendsgiving." To my dismay, however, I was surprised about how much I didn't quite fit in. My autistic traits caused others to see me as odd, "off," or different well before being considered the same. When I tried to join autistic spaces? I often found myself being the only person of color in the room.

While Black and autistic voices are slowly getting more amplified, we are far from heard in both the Black and autistic communities. We have unique challenges, such as police brutality and poor awareness, let alone acceptance. Police brutality is a continuing crisis in the USA and in nations with security concerns such as Nigeria. This crisis is heightened for the African American community as well as the Black, autistic community where autistic individuals can appear and act even more outside of the expected "norm." In addition, autism diagnosis rates are lower for Black people (Centers for Disease Control and Prevention, 2018) not because Black people are unlikely to be autistic, but because most healthcare systems across the world overlook symptoms of autism that aren't presented as the standard clinical and research norm, which is currently Western white males. This leaves Black individuals of all ages excluded from services that can support them as early as infancy. It also leaves us vulnerable to heightened feelings of loneliness, depression, and anxiety.

Community

It took me over two decades of my life to be at peace with my unique differences and to carve out a little community of like-minded individuals. In this book I want to introduce you to several individuals who faced similar challenges. These individuals have come from all parts of the world, including the USA, UK, Canada, Tanzania, South Africa, and Nigeria, with their countries of origin from several more. They are atheist, agnostic, Christian, Muslim, and practicing African Spiritual traditions. Some identified as LG-BTQ+. A couple of individuals spoke to me with eloquence rivaling Obama himself, while others were terser, and some are minimal to nonspeaking and communicated with me through alternative means. Some have children whom they want the best for, while others are still children themselves with dreams of their future ahead. Some are influencers with thousands of followers, while others don't utilize social media at all. Some individuals I physically met before at certain points in my life, and others I met for the very first time on our Google Meet interview. However, every voice in this book is needed for the ongoing conversation of human rights and advocacy, to create awareness of the experiences of a select group of neurodivergent individuals; making the world a better place for all.

Ujima

I want to make a disclaimer that this book is not intended to segregate or enforce identity politics, but to bring previously silenced voices to the conversation. At the end of the day, everyone reading this book is responsible for the well-being and protection of all fellow human beings. By highlighting voices and contributions from this demographic with limited media voices, I hope the subsequent words in this book will bring both awareness and empowerment so that you can advocate for those whom you might not have fully understood previously.

Yes, the primary features of this book will be both Black and autistic, but it was important to the definition of Ujima to not make it fully so. For example, a few individuals in the book have self-diagnosed themselves as autistic, as financial reasons made it limiting to receive a formal diagnosis. Others in the book are nonblack people of color, white, and/or neurotypical. The primary focus of Ujima is in fact "Collective Work and Responsibility" of the entire community, after all. It's never too late to start practicing the principles in Kwanzaa, while it's also time we open the door for previously silenced voices in our communities to be heard.

It took me over two decades to understand the similarities and differences that we all share as humans. It took me even longer to be at peace with the intersectional differences I had myself as a

Black and autistic suburban woman. I hope this book will be a more efficient way for others to come to this understanding as I did.

The book is composed of three parts that entail three or four sections each. In the first section, you will meet individuals who are learning to love themselves. In the second section, you will meet individuals who are overcoming harsh realities such as police brutality and extreme stigma. The third section, sometimes split in two, features individuals advocating for the protection and acceptance of themselves and their fellow humans.

The sections or chapters in each part will be followed by commentary from me with my personal experience learning to better love myself and others in various parts of the world.

Through Ujima, I hope to do my best to highlight the challenges and intersectionalities of human conditions like autism by zeroing in on the Black experience. I hope to bring forward our pain points and celebrate the triumphs of Black autistics as well as family members and organizations that care for these individuals. Through following the real stories of these individuals around the world, I hope fellow Black and autistic individuals will be empowered to realize that being Black and autistic is enough. For those who may not be either Black or autistic, I hope we can all learn to better accept and advocate for marginalized voices across the world. Finally, I hope being vulnerable about my personal experience of being both a perpetrator and victim of "othering" will guide and encourage you along your journeys of awareness, acceptance, and forgiveness.

I hope we can all be reminded to provide respect and a platform for silenced voices in our lives. It's both needed and beneficial for us all:

Through Community.

Through Ujima.

Always.

Part 1
Growth

Chapter 1
Biding Time

Birmingham, England • Harvard University, Massachusetts, USA

Olivia Brown
Birmingham, England

"Not guilty," was the final verdict. The lead juror's words jolted Olivia into a whirlwind of thoughts. Her world, which at the moment was the courtroom, spun as well. A black cloud seemed to emerge, leaving others' reactions and final words inaudible.

Her attacker was found "not guilty." She was found "unreliable," and that was all she needed to hear to understand that she was, once again, deeply and severely misunderstood.

As always, Olivia had no choice but to get up. The clouded room choked her, silencing her from speaking to her family or lawyer. She took one deep breath, then another, and one more. The emotional cloud dissipated as she took her final steps out of the courtroom. She'd hoped that would be the case. However, a second cloud quickly emerged in its place, a less common one, and one more difficult to explain. She feared this cloud.

Her hands flapped. Softly at first, like the pedestrians minding their business on the pavement. Gradually, her arms moved like the British cyclists abruptly swerving to their bike lane across the street. Then, Olivia's voice came back, louder than the horns of the irritated vehicles making way. Olivia told me how she "erupted" into stims and wails made from overstimulation.

"My world came crashing down," Olivia said, "and I was completely 'unhinged'." She recounted that, outside of the courtroom, most police officers were afraid of her stims coupled with her emotional turmoil. They came not to her aid, but to protect her attacker and others from her reaction. As they approached, however, they feared for themselves instead. One officer called for backup, then another, as Olivia continued her meltdown. The original cloud began to re-emerge as Olivia's fear grew stronger. Before she knew it, she was on the ground. She still screamed and wailed, while the officers still didn't know how to approach her. Pedestrians, cyclists, and vehicle onlookers began to take notice as Olivia could not break free from the cloud's grip.

Finally, a Grenadian security guard pulled Olivia up and stroked her hair. The Black security guard pulled her close until her breathing slowed, and the cloud vanished.

A few days later, Olivia relayed her trauma to an older family friend who also had a negative experience with the police in his youth. With ackee, saltfish, and fried dumpling on the cooker, Olivia's friend reminded her about slave rebellions on the ships during the transatlantic slave trade. He told her how the revolts on the ships were more likely to happen when there were more enslaved women onboard. In the book *Wake: The Hidden History of Women-Led Slave Revolts* (2022), the author Dr. Rebecca Hall noted that enslaved women were less likely to be chained or tied onboard compared to men. The women who led these revolts had to wait to act when it was most appropriate to make their move. In her case, Olivia wanted to create an advocacy initiative when it was the most appropriate time for her to do so.

"Biding time," Olivia said, recalling what her family friend told her. "They were biding their time. So I should also bide my time, and wait for the right time of resistance to successfully rebel." Her friend reminded her to follow the enslaved women's lead and not lash out rashly. She didn't know it yet, but she had a community to form to help create change in England. Olivia explained to me how the Black Grenadian security guard was the perfect example of what community policing is. "We need a cultural understanding for all races and neurotypes. But, until then, we need to bide our time and have more public officials from diverse ethnic groups, and we all should support them." The Grenadian security guard, Olivia knew, understood that she was afraid to end up like many Black autistic individuals before her. As her family friend once was, Olivia was scared of being fatally restrained due to being perceived as a threat.

"In this predominantly white area, it was the connection to my culture that was important to me. While I didn't always remember to follow that advice, biding my time when I did is what ultimately saved me."

When conducting Olivia's interview, it was as if she and I were looking in a mirror—in both experiences and in facial expressions. Our mirrored expressions reflected a barrier we imposed on understanding both ourselves and each other. Oblivious to our mirrored personas, I asked Olivia to take me back to the beginning. Unlike the courthouse, it was time for Olivia to be given the opportunity to explain her hopes, her dreams, and who she is as a human being. Afterwards, I figured I'd prioritize asking her how to spell the word ackee.

Olivia's values came from the sum of her life experiences, loving family, and Jamaican cultural heritage. She didn't seem to fit in multiple worlds, and would later come to realize that it was also a neurotypical point of view. For example, Olivia expressed what she later came to realize as her first memory of having sensory sensitivities. Before she slept, she needed her room to be a satisfactory level of both cool and dark.

"The curtains needed to be black-out curtains. There needed to be a fan angling directly at me, and of course, I needed white noise to sleep peacefully."

Olivia was quick to readjust her environment to suit her sensory needs. An independent, precocious girl, she was ready to take any challenge head on, and readjust it to fit her desired routine as needed. Little did she know that in British secondary school, of course, that challenge was not sensory-related, but mean-girl-related. To make matters worse, Olivia felt like she was the only Jamaican Black British person in the world who didn't imbed patois or a hint of the accent into her speech. For her, it was a recipe for alienation, a lifelong situation she tolerated more for herself than for her vulnerable peers around her.

"I found that neurotypical children were forming cliques, and bullying was taking place," Olivia said while shaking her head. "It bothered me so much, so I started to stand up for the kids who were getting bullied. Hoping to get us all back to a sense of our previous childhood normality." I nodded in commiseration, anticipating what was next to come. "Which unfortunately made me the target. I had a few run-ins with the popular group because of this." The increase in complex social systems, such as cliques and bullying, makes the transition between primary (elementary) and secondary school a challenging task for Olivia and autistic girls like her (Sedgewick, Hill, & Pellicano, 2018). For Olivia, she felt safer remaining an advocate, albeit a loner one.

"Someone's gotta stick up for those being attacked. Why not me." Turns out, Olivia's not alone in this thinking. Studies show that autistic individuals have a stronger sense of justice and stricter adherence to what's right and wrong compared to non-autistic individuals (Hu *et al.*, 2021). Olivia cared so much about her vulnerable classmates that she repeatedly put herself in harm's way of the mean girls to protect them. However, the long-term impact of standing up for these bully survivors and the repercussions it caused her was traumatic and left her with mental health problems for years to come.

So how did this all affect you? I asked.

"I was frankly unable to get over it until maybe like five years ago," Olivia said. With severe mental health outcomes prevailing in autistics at significantly higher rates than neurotypicals, she's unfortunately not alone (Jones *et al.*, 2014). Countless research, case studies, and anecdotal blog posts show autistic individuals reporting high rates of trauma and abuse in schools. In a viral post, Dr. Marcia Eckerd discusses how the current school system is designed to ostracize autistic students (Eckerd, 2021).

Olivia made do with her tight-knit caring community of mostly her mom, brother, and a sage family friend. While sourcing the ingredients for traditional Jamaican "Satdeh" (Saturday) soup in Birmingham, England was relatively easy, Olivia teetered the line between fitting in among her white British neighbors, feeling alienated among her classmates, and being confused by the societal standards that were imposed on her as a middle-class citizen.

The class structure, such as the middle class, is very stark and ingrained in one's location, accent, and many other defining features. While it made her one of the only Black people in her immediate area, she did enjoy privileges that many of her Black British counterparts did not experience.

"Fortunately, my mom really catered to my needs; even before she knew why I had those needs. I was able to bide my time at GCSE [General Certificate of Secondary Education]," she said, still without losing focus on eye contact. Olivia's mom scheduled regular massages for her to help with her stress, and their family even moved houses across town for her to be closer to her school.

"The commute started to get taxing for me. I was feeling overloaded," she stated, acknowledging that her classmates probably considered her to be nothing other than spoiled. Outside of her affluent, middle-class area, the assumptions persisted of her being entitled and undeserving of the accommodation her family allotted her. That is until A-levels at sixth form became the turning point to discover the underlying cause of her talents and hurdles so far.

The sixth form or college is a British educational stage two years before enrolling in university. For these youth generally between 16 and 18 years old, they begin to specialize in a few chosen subjects or a trade apprenticeship. As a 16-year-old, Olivia found the transition to college very difficult. The demographics and social class of her classmates changed, and she was unaccustomed to an under-resourced school environment that she felt allowed for a high proportion of disruptive students and those that she felt did not value their education.

"I really didn't like change," she said. "Making friends, making projects, making eye contact…it was all so hard for me to do then." I noted the irony of her current overabundance of eye contact with me. She described her visceral experience of mental distress as her "brain seeping through her ears", overwhelming her as she struggled to memorize content that she once did successfully during GCSEs.

She came home from college one day, exhausted as usual. A second sage family friend was over, talking to her mom in the family room above the aroma of brown stew chicken. Olivia gave her usual sigh and when her family friend heard, they asked her what was wrong. To the friend's surprise, Olivia could not stay and converse because she had to run to her room to rid herself of her uncomfortable clothes, all before taking some deep breaths in the quietness of her retreat. When Olivia returned, her family friend's conversation grew more hushed and concerned.

"Autism," was the word Olivia overheard muttered occasionally. When she joined the conversation, the three of them confirmed it may be the term that made her sensory and social dilemmas finally make sense. When the conversation began to become overwhelming, Olivia retreated to her room again to take a brief online screening quiz and was amazed that she matched all of the classic screening symptoms.

"Well, except one," she said in our interview, looking at me slightly off to the side of my screen, giving me a chance to take a satisfying blink before I rejoined my imagined staring competition. I didn't have time to ponder the reasoning or implication of our staring contest before she resumed.

The 16-year-old Olivia soon consulted her doctor or general practitioner (GP), who was dismissive. "He said I'm too intelligent to have anything wrong with me. I should just work on what I'm good at, and go away," Olivia said while shaking her head.

Franckie Castro-Ramirez
Harvard University, Massachusetts, USA

"I'm not surprised by all this," Franckie Castro-Ramirez, a psychology Ph.D. student at Harvard University, said in a separate conversation. Leaning back and nodding in her chair as if she heard similar situations before, Castro-Ramirez studies clinical psychology, specifically, the disparities in mental health as it relates to self- and other-directed violence. She is the first author of an internationally renowned journal article titled "Racism and poverty are the barriers to the treatment of youth mental health concern" (Castro-Ramirez et al., 2021), but explained to me that she didn't originally set out to write the paper.

"I originally assumed I would write a treatment approach for adolescents with suicidal thoughts and behavior, but I knew that subset was saturated," she said, and, as I worked as a research assistant in her lab years prior, I understood her point. Another article she co-authored, "Understanding the who, why and when of suicide risk" (Nock, Ramirez, & Rankin, 2019), criticized researchers' theoretical approach to understanding suicide, and advocated for new approaches including understanding people's thoughts and behaviors during heightened risk. "I wanted to write something relatively new, so I decided to focus on what mattered to me as a mixed-raced Puerto Rican with ADHD." Castro-Ramirez then gathered Dr. Matthew Nock and her fellow graduate trainees of color to coauthor a paper to discuss the intersection of race and barriers to mental health care.

Castro-Ramirez and her coauthors noted that the barriers were a systemic result of racism. Not only is there a lack of structural access to care for mental health resources and services like culturally informed autism diagnosis, but there are attitudinal barriers, like mistrust in institutions, that may be contributing to the significant lack of Black youth reporting suicidal thoughts compared to white youth. Previous research showed that it was because of fear of being involuntarily hospitalized or taken into police custody, which stems from the ongoing history of police brutality (Anderson, Lowry, & Wuensch, 2015). Castro-Ramirez also reasoned it may be why Black youth learn to mask neurodivergent traits consistent with the autism spectrum.

"It's like, 'why should I trust the system that has experimented on my ancestors and colonized the world...' you know, pretty reasonable right?" One of the final reasons for barriers to care related to Olivia's experience the most: the cultural barriers dividing many clinicians and their clients. In an area where there is more anti-Black racism or ostracism, such as Olivia being one of the only Black individuals in her immediate area of an otherwise diverse city, the effectiveness of care decreases in Black youth more than in any other race (Price et al., 2020). With nearly 70 percent of doctoral-trained clinical psychologists identifying as white (National Science Foundation, 2019), and many of them overworked with a full client list, the odds of a Black youth experiencing medical gaslighting, invalidations and not being understood are perceived by many youths to be quite high.

Olivia Brown
Birmingham, England

While Olivia's GP was dismissive, she was lucky in that he did reluctantly refer her to a cognitive behavioral therapist. However, her satisfaction didn't last long. She described that the practitioner didn't have an awareness of autism, and was condescending about her sensory difficulties that often become inflamed before menstruation.

"The cognitive-behavioral therapist kept saying: 'It's thoughts that influence feelings, hormones don't play a role.' It's like he couldn't change the way he described how my thoughts influence my feelings in a way that made sense to me. No analogies, no metaphors. Nothing."

Shortly after starting the therapy sessions, Olivia had a breakdown during sixth form (final two years of high school) and had to withdraw temporarily. Noticing the severity of the situation, her mom helped her transfer to a different doctor who was recommended by a family friend. Fortunately, that doctor was much more empathetic and agreed with Olivia and her family's perspective on autism. The doctor referred her to a diagnostic center.

The United Kingdom has a notoriously long waitlist for receiving an autism diagnosis, with the average wait time rumored to be around 2–3 years. Many, like Olivia, struggle to get a referral because they do not meet the presentation of symptoms consistent with white people on the autism spectrum. Autistic women and people of color are impacted the hardest by these outdated stereotypes regarding autism (Aylward, Gal-Szabo, & Taraman, 2021). England's National Health Service (NHS) reported that over 77 percent receive their first appointment at least 13 weeks after a referral (NHS, 2022). Originally, Olivia was scheduled to journey 300 miles to Scotland to have the assessment conducted in two and a half years' time. Fortunately, a rare cancellation in a nearby center emerged, shortening her journey by just over 290 miles, and her wait time was shortened to six months.

Weeks after her appointment, Olivia was finally diagnosed with autism spectrum disorder. She was overwhelmed with a sense of relief, but also grief at the amount of time she had lost not truly understanding herself and feeling out of place and behind her classmates who she continued to feel isolated from. This a truly relatable feeling for myself and many autistics like us. She received disability accommodations in sixth form but attitudinal barriers from teachers prevented them from being effective. Her mental health plunged again and Olivia left for the final time. Her mom attempted to place her in a specialist further education college in southeast England, but it was far too expensive, and their local governing authority deemed the reasoning behind the transfer unsuitable to fund.

"That really affected my mental health," Olivia said, "Not having a formal education to go into. No formal employment or upward social mobility." She felt that the government and its lack of accommodations for her condition let her down, leaving her with no hope to attain her goals for her future. Olivia fell into a deep depression that resulted in her first suicide attempt at 17 years old.

Additionally, Olivia was blindsided by the fact that, despite receiving a diagnosis, many clinicians she went to didn't understand what autism was. Olivia introduced me to the term "diagnostic overshadowing". Meaning that her practitioners often denied her mental health care because her anxiety, depression, and suicidality symptoms did not resonate with them as separate traits of autism.

"It's like they just see autism and not what's around it," she said.

I scratched my head on the other side of the interview screen. I've been fortunate enough to not have severe anxiety or depression spells since being diagnosed with autism, so the diagnostic overshadowing term was admittedly hard for me to comprehend. After finding further research that this is a prevalent result of many diagnoses, whether physical, mental, or neurodevelopmental (Hollocks et al., 2019), I asked Castro-Ramirez how this phenomenon fits into her research.

Frankie Castro-Ramirez
Harvard University, Massachusetts, USA

"Not surprised again," Castro-Ramirez said, regarding Olivia's experience. Castro-Ramirez described how she noticed in her research and own life how Black and Brown autistic youth are often scolded and disciplined much more harshly than others. Most of the time, the scolding occurs without considering the root cause of their symptoms. Many autistic youths, especially Black boys and girls, are often misdiagnosed as having disruptive behavior disorders—even when having received an autism diagnosis (NPR, 2018). The implications of this will be discussed later in this book.

Olivia Brown
Birmingham, England

Olivia continued to experience her mental health challenges when she was 18. Without being able to pursue an education through a university at that time, she decided to pursue a career in marketing. While she found her employer insensitive to her accommodation needs, she became passionate about a subset of her field called arts marketing. She developed a burgeoning new special interest in the arts and began to attend art galleries regularly.

"I found a sense of achievement, sense of progress," she said, referring to an arts marketing course for young adults that she enrolled in at the time. While her eyes were still glued to mine, I imagined her wanting to look off to the side, pleased with the fond memory of her formative years. I quickly found that I was mistaken, however, as Olivia described a heinous event that occurred right when she felt her life was about to fall into place.

"All of the hard work I did to find my passion and to dig myself out of depression and anxiety, it was all set back," Olivia said, describing how, two years into her arts marketing pursuit, she became a survivor of rape by the hands of a man she was dating. Oliva reported the incident, but she was quickly retraumatized by testifying to a doubtful jury. While Olivia went through the stress of having to relive her experience by retelling her assault, the jurors' decision was one rooted in ignorance of different cultures and neurotypes.

It was then that Olivia consulted with her family friend who had a negative experience with the police. Like her ancestors before her, Olivia needed to summon up her patience and will and bide her time. However, the pressure for a young adult to be that strong in the face of unprecedented turmoil was too great. It was then that she decided to try to bide her time by self-medicating.

She felt pushed over the edge when the verdict found her attacker not guilty. Leading up to and during the trial, she began smoking marijuana as a coping mechanism. The quantity and frequency increased. Hours, then days, blurred into one. After the trial, Olivia was so reliant on smoking that she started developing psychosis.

"I fervently believed I was the rightful heir to the crown," Olivia said, in her usual "posh" British, patois-less demeanor. "The throne. The English throne," she politely added, probably after noticing my confusion. "I also believed I was the granddaughter of the former emperor of Ethiopia, and even Jesus at one point. So yeah, in hindsight I had what is known as delusions of grandeur."

One afternoon she went to confront her family friend based on her delusions. Olivia's delusions shocked her guest so much that they called the police. She was then taken to a mental health institution for the first time in her life and was overwhelmed with sensory overload. As usual, Olivia needed her room to be dark and quiet while sleeping. However, like most inpatient units, nurses and care workers frequently came in with torchlights to do routine checks and shone it in her face, triggering her light sensitivity. With the contradiction, she became impatient and often argued with one of the lead nurses.

"[The nurse] biggest offense was that she almost didn't let my mom bring me my favorite lotion for me to use after I showered," Olivia said. "Black people need lotion!" She later noted that her actual biggest offense was the nurse purposefully making her miss a meal. Her aggression with the nurse eventually became so much that staff restrained her and sent her to a seclusion room, where her lotion was confiscated. In a sensory nightmare with dry, itchy skin, Olivia only became more aggressive. Her mom and family friends once again became the aid in giving her the help that she needed. Behind the walls of seclusion, they slowly taught her coping mechanisms for her to calm herself and feel better. Her mom advocated for her release, which wasn't provided for a total of ten days—eight of which were spent in seclusion.

Franckie Castro-Ramirez
Harvard University, Massachusetts, USA

Olivia's life post-diagnosis mirrored the research Franckie Castro-Ramirez wrote on behalf of all neurodivergent youth of color. When I asked Castro-Ramirez how the psychological research community reacted to her barriers to treatment article, she shrugged and sighed. "Well...it's been quiet. It hasn't been good enough. The field can and should be having a better response to the mental health crisis brought on by systemic racism. I mean, you know...these papers out there and it's like, chasing the wind. Right now I'm a graduate student, so the little power I have is in the papers I choose to write. We need advocates out there and we need more and better support for those who are doing the work in schools, hospitals, and communities." Castro-Ramirez's words from Harvard University not only resonated with me but our communities at large. While Castro-Ramirez never met Olivia, much less engaged with her, it was clear that Olivia felt similarly through her subsequent actions and goals.

Olivia Brown
Birmingham, England

In Birmingham, England, Olivia walked out of the inpatient hospital with a sense of resolve to continue to advocate for herself. She enrolled in a university program to formally pursue Critical Autism Studies and created the popular Twitter handle @BlackAutistics. Olivia shares her own experiences, learns from others, and shares knowledge with people outside of the Black and autistic community. She enjoys what she's doing to help people like her, and, despite the challenges, she still feels mostly relief and comfort from receiving her autism diagnosis. While the reality is that there will always be hurdles in her long life ahead, Olivia has a community—both familial and online—and her determination to make her life one well lived.

Toward the end of our interviews, Olivia took a deep exhale. She looked at me through the lens of her webcam, from the Google Meet tab on my screen. Stoic. She confidently tried to gather my facial expression as she concluded her life story with me. Smugly, I assumed, like many people before her, that she wouldn't be able to make out what I was thinking this time. I assumed she would look away. Down. Behind. To the left. Anything.

Per usual, Olivia didn't do any of those. She remained stoic. Eyes steady, lips and expression flat. Confidence. Mirroring my expression to the tee. As she was my first interviewee, I wasn't used to hearing someone with such a similar story and background as mine. For so long, I had felt alone in the world, that the thought of someone out there having the same struggles and experiences as mine was cathartic, albeit awkward to witness an emotional doppelganger.

Flustered, I put my hand behind my head, refusing to break eye contact. I mentally scanned through my notes one more time to see if there were any more follow-up questions to ask. When I was satisfied, I shrugged, eyes still locked on hers.

"So, what's next?" I asked. Noticing that the two of us, locking eyes with each other, refusing to blink or fidget, was a form of masking.

Why? I thought, *did two Black autistic people still feel the need to mask?* After feeling so alone, misunderstood, and tired for so long, perhaps the longing to be accepted and display genuine understanding and appreciation is hard to do. Especially for late-diagnosed Black women like ourselves. It was evidence that differences in class, race, and neurotypes from our peers made both of us hypervigilant about being outed as "not enough" at any point in time, including during this conversation.

It was then that I realized that, to break the cycle of hypervigilance and stress in the Black autistic community, we need to trust each other that deep down, we'll have each other's back. We'll understand. We'll do the work to learn more about our community as well as those different from ours. To do that, we both needed to relax, be ourselves and truly open up. I made a note to do that in all subsequent conversations with those that would share similar unique experiences with me.

I blinked. I smiled. And then I chuckled when I realized that Olivia did too at the same time. I rejoiced at the revelation we seemingly quietly shared, and was optimistic for the interviews with others ahead. I felt ambitious about the work and advocacy needed for all of us to continue to heal and thrive. I was proud of her for taking that leap on Twitter.

Olivia leaned back in her chair for the first time in our virtual meetings. I made a mental note of her extended stay at the psychiatric hospital, her prolonged court case, her experience of being ostracised in secondary school, and all the patience she had no choice but to show. The resilience she developed. Through the seemingly never-ending cycle of racism, sexism, and ableism.

"What now?" I repeated, marveling at her grace.

Olivia let her eye contact falter, and a half-smile emerged on her lips.

"You know," she said, "the usual. Biding my time."

Ujima
Okinawa, Japan

I never got the solo part in my school's choir. To be fair, I was 12 years old, and at the ripe age where I didn't understand that I was completely tone deaf. As the daughter of an army officer, I spent many humid nights and clear blue sky days rehearsing the solo to "American Tears" on Japan's tropical island of Okinawa, home to Kadena Air Base. We moved several times before, but my years in Japan were the pinnacle for cultivating what I loved thus far. At our elementary school, I was known as the girl of niche talents. Those talents included, but were not limited to:

- digging up and reburying pretty rocks
- writing long, dramatic song lyrics, screenplays, and short stories
- being the undefeated champion of foot races at recess
- somehow locating and training the fastest snail (yes, snail) in our neighborhood bug races.

So yeah, I had a lot of pressure to keep the momentum going. I was also named Student Body President of our elementary school. Primarily for my snail stardom, but also because I promised the school that I would increase recess and lunch (which maybe played a small factor). With the new groupies I gained after my inauguration, I had a small crowd come to see my solo audition.

I wasn't used to having people surround me, as the fans were often sparse in rock collecting and snail racing. In the choir room after school, however, my presidential groupies gave me a thumbs-up as I approached the microphone. In the three-walled room under the ocean-blue clear island sky, I took one last breath before beginning the final verse of "American Tears."

What I remember most about my singing abilities back then was that I was an alto that desperately wanted to be a soprano. I'm sure it showed that day as the groupies looked at each other before running out of the door, most likely to laugh, but at the time I wondered if they were in awe.

A few months later, as a sage 12½-year-old, I clapped for the girl who did get the solo of "American Tears." Fortunately, my claps weren't audible to our small audience, as I clapped from the furthest spot from the microphone that I was assigned to, of course. I assumed that I would get a solo the next year, or at my subsequent school in the next country we lived. Like Olivia, however, my life wouldn't be as linear as I would have assumed. For one, I also assumed I would continue to develop my passion for writing, but it would take a rollercoaster worth of years of experience for me to decide to pick it back up.

Olivia's life mirrored mine in more ways than one. When she was interviewed, I assumed she would reveal that she had a sign that she was autistic since infancy. For Olivia and myself, the traits that resembled niche-interest girlhood were the traits that would define our trials in our teenage and adult years to come. Awkward girlhoods were hard to isolate from other slightly less awkward ones, especially in the 1990s.

Similar to Olivia as well, one thing in my life did remain consistent from my non-existent solo choir days; opportunities and "groupies" did not come easy. It was going to be an uphill battle to make friends (much less keep them) and succeed in school, work, and other relationships. After discovering the word autism as an adult, it wouldn't be too long before both of us realized that we needed to be twice as good to achieve half as much in the aforementioned aspects, primarily because of our race, gender, and neurotype.

Our niche interests, values, and personalities as autistic individuals need to be listened to and explored in the communication form that we present. For Black autistics specifically, both stereotyping and misunderstandings of ourselves by others can be dangerous, as Ndumi and James will express in the next chapter. For Olivia, however, her interests and passions needed time to present themselves to her first, as life had some hurdles in the way before she found her footing. For those, like Olivia, who have a slow start or a bumpy ride, it's important to remember that even the lowest-ranked snail in the neighbourhood bug race would ultimately make it to the finish line. I'm so thankful she kept moving.

Chapter 2
The Rhythm of Our Times

Gauteng, South Africa • Detroit, Michigan, USA • Windsor, Ontario, Canada

Ndumi
Gauteng, South Africa

In Gauteng, South Africa, ten-year-old Ndumi approached the computer screen when we connected on Google Meet. To my surprise, Ndumi's face came closer and closer, until Tracy softly ushered him back to his seat. Before he did so, he pressed his head to the screen, and hands to the keyboard once more before making sounds. His mother sat patiently in a seat in the background while I introduced myself to him again. I explained to him that I was writing a book on Black autistic people just like him, and that he had the privilege of being the youngest member interviewed. Ndumi made more sounds. Tracy, noticing my calm, let Ndumi get back to his seat on his own. Ndumi made a few more sounds and expressions before smiling and backing away to his seat. Like many children, he was distracted by the world around him, and fascinated by it all. Ndumi smiled and used his letterboard to spell out his spoken dialogue.

"Hi, Kala," he said, "I'm so excited to be a part of your book."

As the screen was mirrored, and as I did not yet have the under-standing to fully communicate through a letterboard, Tracy verbal-ized Ndumi's answers for the duration of the interview. Ndumi is nonspeaking and uses his spelling board to communicate. Ndumi, his mother, and I, moderated by his speech therapist Tracy, dis-cussed the trials and triumphs in his young life.

When asked about his favorite hobby, Ndumi said he enjoyed play-ing on his iPad. He specifically loves his screen to watch history and science documentaries, and, of course, to play video games. He lives with his parents and two younger siblings. When I enquired if he enjoys sharing the joy of his iPad with his siblings or friends he told me how he had trouble communicating things he loved with those outside of his mind.

"Not normally," he said in response to my question. "It's tough to share when you can't speak."

While I was waiting for Ndumi's responses, I noticed how Tracy was gently encouraging Ndumi to move on to pointing the let-ters on the letterboard. She would say "And" in between each letter, sometimes multiple times, such as "I. And. Love. And. And. My. And. And. I Love. My. And. And. iPad." The use of the letter-board has stemmed from the International Association for Spelling and Communication (I-ASC), a group that consists of nonspeak-ing and neurodiverse individuals like Ndumi, their families, in this case Ndumi's mom, and clinical practitioners, like Tracy. The goal is for the parties to come together to ensure that nonspeaking individuals have the autonomy that they deserve through the use of a letterboard. To start, the I-ASC ensures that communica-tion is effective across the three parties (I-ASC, n.d.). Then, finally, nonspeaking children, teens, and adults alike will have the tools needed to communicate effectively with the rest of their community and the world at large.

I observed that the black letterboard consisted of five rows of four letters alphabetically, with the top and bottom rows consisting of five letters. Ndumi discussed with me some points where he witnessed others being nice to him, and others being mean.

"I find acceptance at home and in my school. I have friends just like me at school that make my life great," he said, and I smiled. Ndumi got up to pace a bit before proceeding, "It would be a better world if people understood autism better."

Every time Ndumi goes outside, people stare or make rude comments. "Like, 'what's wrong with him?'" Ndumi elaborated. Overwhelmed, Ndumi got up to go lay on his mom's lap in the back of the office. His mom smiled and stroked him briefly before he came back to proceed. When I later followed up with his mom about those that stared at him, she said that she has seen people get scared of Ndumi sometimes and that it makes her aware that people don't understand autism.

Ndumi's emotional reaction was more apparent. He said that he has noticed that people are afraid of him and that he's worried that it would get worse as he gets "bigger." Ndumi's mannerisms, sudden movements, and sounds, along with stimming to self-soothe and process emotions, are all factors that make a growing Black boy stand out even among those like him. In South Africa's past and current oppression of Black individuals, he fears he could stand out as a target around those who hold more social power or force over him.

"I'm not sure why they see me as scary." He added, "I am so soft and gentle inside. When I sense fear in people I want to cry. It is so unfair to judge me without knowing or understanding me first. I hope other autistics don't have this too."

Ndumi got up to move closer to the screen before turning to Tracy. He touched her forehead before leaning in for a hug. Tracy accepted the hug, both of their shoulders softening during the brief embrace. I asked Ndumi what else he'd like to tell others about himself, and he concluded with: "The hardest part of my life was when I had no voice. I worry about all the nonspeakers still trapped in a prison of silence. It keeps me up at night."

For Ndumi, being able to communicate with the spelling board opened doors for him in that others were finally able to listen to him and get to know his personality better. For those that put in the effort to listen and understand him, like those at school for example, they're able to be gifted with a kind and funny boy who, like his counterparts, enjoys the world around him and wants others to enjoy it with him.

One example of his enjoyment is his endearment to all subjects in school, and his propensity to take on more challenging subjects. "I like them all. But math is my best," Ndumi said, right after getting up to hug his mom. Ndumi's mom chuckled when he discussed how he didn't have a pet, but would love to be allowed to adopt a cat one day. Curious, I asked if cats were his favorite animal. To my surprise, Ndumi said that elephants were. He elaborated that they were his favorite because they were silent and intelligent, just like him. I witnessed Ndumi note my previous perplexion. Like most children, he felt a duty to explain to an oblivious adult like me why he wouldn't want to adopt an elephant and instead settle for a cat. Forlorn, Ndumi typed in his letterboard for a few seconds to clarify.

Tracy's gentle "And"s were all that broke the brief silence. I smiled at Ndumi's clarification:

"Unfortunately, Kala, elephants won't fit in my room."

James Mosely
Detroit, Michigan, USA • Windsor, Ontario, Canada

A 1990 TV show debut was the moment James prepared for all of his life on the US–Canadian border. Well, for about ten years, as he had been performing since he was four years old. People age out quickly in show business after all. James and his brother (his dance partner) were to appear on the first episode of "Speakers Corner", a popular Canadian show at the time. The two of them danced like no one was watching, although a lot of the country was. After the performance, the pair were escorted out, and were met with thousands of screaming fans.

"I felt like a superstar, to say the least," James recalled to me, refer-ring to the flashing lights of the fans and media as they exited the debut. While Ndumi is nonspeaking, James considers himself to be minimally speaking. He has significant trouble speaking with-out substantial preparation. James also does not own a cell phone, as he finds it more difficult than speaking audibly. "I can feel the electromagnetic energy from them. It burns," he says. Given this, I opted to communicate with James over email to hear his story. He's also a friend of Jason Cathcart (featured in the next chapter) who provided more context beforehand.

Back in Canada several decades ago, however, young James felt guilty that he could no longer locate one of the staff members in the room. He realized that he officially got her fired.

Earlier that evening, James was parched in the green room on set. He needed water, but, as a young teenager, James didn't yet understand the dynamics of show business. So instead of requesting someone to provide bottled water for him, he simply attempted to leave the room to drink from a water fountain. Hands on her hips, one of the production assistants stood in front of the door, looked him straight in the eyes, and said, "I can't let you go out there."

"I demanded to be able to get my own water, even though the woman called down for cases of water and food," James said. When the production assistant's boss heard James raise his voice, the boss immediately went up to her and fired her for upsetting their young guest.

James was taken aback. For the first time in his young life, he realized the power his actions and words could have on others. James learned that not every hands-on-hip adult was out to get him, and he needed to empathize and understand the humanity behind the adult. As a teenager, he had to let go of his previous bias that every adult existed to withhold or take away something from him. As a performer, the power imbalance between him and those behind the scenes was drastic, and he had a responsibility to protect those who worked for him.

"From that day forward I chose my words carefully when on my job," James stated. Shortly after the debut, he apologized to the TV station and insisted that the production assistant did nothing wrong. Unfortunately for her, she never was reinstated, and James later learned that she had no choice but to leave expensive Toronto and start afresh.

At 13, James promised himself that he wouldn't hurt another member of his community again. Unfortunately, there were harmful people in his community who used their power to do just that to him and more.

James witnessed multiple events of police brutality in his life. He grew up traveling frequently between inner-city Detroit, Michigan, USA, and Windsor, Ontario, Canada across the river. He witnessed and experienced police brutality in both locations. James also has a spectacular memory where he can remember details of his life from as early as toddlerhood. It's useful when he recalls several amazing memories of his childhood but could be traumatizing when recalling those memories that were prevalent during his time on both sides of the river.

A child in his neighborhood got a gun and played with it. He accidentally shot himself in the abdomen and was bleeding out. A family friend of James picked the boy up and ran him to the hospital.

"Ambulances weren't allowed to show up without police presence at the time in Detroit and cops didn't care about the hood, so it was best to walk or run to the hospital," James informed me.

In the end, the police were eventually called. The police looked at the bleeding child, and the distraught adult, and saw the zipcode on their form. The police immediately arrested the family friend, and he ended up spending ten years in jail for being at the wrong place at the wrong time. As James got older, it baffled him how people in predominantly white areas were given the benefit of the doubt by the police. From drug usage to loud parties, to simply trying to help a young neighbor, James carried these memories with him to form his belief that being Black was deadly.

James lived in a low-income housing development where drive-by shootings and violence were ordinary. At a young age, he found several guns in their community trash bin and later found out that they were used for multiple armed robberies, leaving one innocent person dead.

In environments like this, it's difficult for all members of a nuclear family to make it to adulthood without being shot or arrested. Fortunately for James, his parents were very protective of him and his siblings. They tried to expose them to the world outside of the hood as much as they could. His parents also sought to lay down their own lives for James and his siblings' safety at all costs.

Bullets were fired at their family when James was barely three years old. James and his family were in their car inching closer to the building where his grandmother lived. Bullets were firing so close to their car and in their direction, it froze James and his siblings. Fortunately, his father acted quickly. He demanded them to lie down in the back of the van, and his father laid himself on top of the young children to shield them from the possible deadly bullets. Through a small gap, with the help of the illuminated street lights, James saw the passing bullets sparking. Thanks to his dad, they all eventually made it into his grandmother's house alive. It turned out that the police were in a shootout with the neighbors. The lives of James and his family were collateral that both parties were apparently willing to risk.

James received the most protection from his dad, who he has recently come to suspect is also autistic. His dad cultivated his love for science and anything that had to do with knowledge. Looking back, James realized he was hyperlexic, as he was able to read full medical journals by the age of four. His parents and teachers worked to keep him occupied and engaged in the special interest he had in knowledge.

While in the first grade in Canada, James was offered a scholarship to what he remembers as a "special school". With the Canadian system allowing students to earn medical degrees in undergrad, the school young James nearly enrolled him in would have set him on track to complete an MD by 16. His parents decided to decline due to the bad history Canada had with residential schools. In mid-2022, for example, the Pope traveled to Alberta to give a formal apology to Canada's indigenous community for the sexual and physical abuse children endured at the hands of the Catholic church (Horowitz, 2022). Nevertheless, young James had more than enough stimulation and fulfillment by continuing to read medical journals, and engaging in his second special interest: dance.

James received payment to dance at only four years old. He danced on both sides of the Detroit River, meaning he danced for both Americans and Canadians alike. At one point, he and his brother were sponsored by Coca-Cola, allowing them to engage more as business partners than brothers at Speakers Corner for most of his teen years.

Despite the young boys' wealth and fame, their parents wanted to continue to reside in the poor areas in Canada and the United States. Their status didn't shield them from the bias and confrontation James continued to experience with the police in Detroit. As a local sensation, James felt responsible for making the mistake he made that got the production assistant fired. However, James wondered why some police officers didn't feel responsible to protect and serve his community, rather he often saw many abuse them, while others stood back and watched.

As an undiagnosed autistic, James had a reputation for speaking bluntly to authority, whether it was by correcting poor grammar, or standing up for someone who was bullied or abused. As one could imagine, it got him in trouble when James approached the police. As James watched some police officers harass his fellow Black citizens in Detroit, James would shout at them and notify them of all the rights they were violating.

"A few times they had enough of my intellect, and would punch me, handcuff me and sit me in the holding cell," James recalled. He said his father would take him home, but not before notifying the police that it's against the law to detain someone for speaking the truth. Unfortunately, not much changed with the relationship between James and the police "It's simply how it was," he said, "and is."

James' childhood came to an end when he became a father at 16. He then had to learn to be the protector and provider for his new family, as his father did for him in his youth. After finishing college, he became a behavior consultant in Canada. As most of his clients were autistic or showed high autistic traits, James deeply understood his clients and thrived. He was able to customize behavior plans and strategies to be effective for his clients. As he worked in the government, he began to see the disparities in the educational system that his excellent test-taking privilege shielded him from in his childhood.

James worked in schools across Canada daily as a consultant but found it extremely upsetting to witness the state of the "special education" programs.

"I wanted things fixed immediately," James said. "No one saw the students as I did. Full of potential and offering so many lessons just by being in their presence. Education is an excellent equalizer, in

my opinion. Allowing anyone to improve the quality of their lives."
James eventually left the position due to burnout and the power-
lessness he felt to bring enough positive change to students who
mirrored his younger self in so many ways.

James eventually started his own behavioral consultancy practice
in Toronto. As the years progressed, James' family expanded to
seven kids, and he noticed that most would socially outgrow him
once they reached puberty. He found it hard to interact with his
children, who also were able to interact with their peers much better than he was able to at their age.

James also struggled with homelessness an unprecedented amount
considering his early success. He became homeless first due to a
split with his first wife, then later as a result of the pandemic. When
asked if his children experienced it with him, James added the following: "So when I began experiencing homelessness, most of my
kids were grown and living on their own. I didn't want to burden
them with my problems but I did confide in my second oldest, Jordan. Of course, he offered to have me stay with him but I didn't
feel it was right. I was afraid whatever my challenges with other
people I'd develop with my son as well. I didn't want that."

James began to ask his behavioral consultancy mentors if they believed he was autistic, and they suggested he receive an assessment outside of the city (as he trained, or trained with, many behavioral consultants in Toronto).

After a tough process, James was diagnosed with autism spectrum
disorder at 41 years old. "Given the intensity of my memories, I tend
to avoid going any deeper into my diagnosis," James said regarding

the assessment. "I found the process extremely difficult [for me] mentally." He quickly became an inspiration in the behavioral consultancy community.

"There's much more to autism than they realize. [When they found out I was autistic] I became the perfect example for them. A family man, business owner, and world traveler. I can't complain at all and others see me as able to provide a powerful testimony on behalf of the capabilities of those on the spectrum. I assure folks, we are all unique. With strengths and weaknesses just like any living creature," James said.

His relationship with his brother and former dancing business partner, however, has gotten more distant, especially since he doesn't believe that James is autistic. "[It's] as if no one believes the words I say," James recalled. "[Which is] another thing about my particular autism, I don't lie." James recounted the time a caseworker instructed him to lie to her coworkers about his condition due to difficulties that James would like to keep private. When he refused, the government refused to provide him with financial support. He became homeless for the third time because of it. He joins up to 12 percent of homeless people who display autistic traits (Churchard et al., 2019). With Black individuals in general accounting for the overwhelming majority of the homeless population in the USA (National Alliance to End Homelessness, 2020), it would be wise to be concerned about the percentage of those who are both Black and autistic. It is imperative for future researchers to one day showcase this as an empirical fact.

At 47, James lives with his wife of seven years. While he struggled to cultivate platonic relationships, he's enjoyed his marriage through the ups and downs. "She has severe anxiety so in some ways we can understand the challenges we both face so we can hold our family together, most of the time," he said, adding a smile emoji at the end. James still battles homelessness and police brutality.

Whenever he looks at one of his dance albums, he's reminded of his album release party when he was 25. In the year 2000, he hosted the pay-to-attend party at the University of Windsor. However, the police refused to let his neighbors in because they recognized them. "The cops knew all of the Black kids because they harassed us all. My friends demanded to get in because they purchased tickets weeks in advance. The pigs beat them at the front door and I thought my folks would be shot dead just for coming to support me," he said.

Ultimately, James is saddened when he continues to get punched and kicked by police in his middle age for his "mouth." However, he never takes it personally with an officer as many would in his situation. "I've never had any issues with individual cops because I understand they are only acting on orders from above. They are trying to feed their families like everyone else. My issue is with the lawmakers, the politicians, and 'elite' who keep racist policies in place," he said. He reminds himself that things need to be reviewed, just like how he became more tolerant of adults as a young teenager all those years ago as an elite dancer. "Nothing will change unless the policies are changed. As policies begin to change, the mindsets of the people following those policies will change, including cops." For now, he continues to do his best to maintain a wonderful life with his wife during the rhythm of these times.

James and Ndumi were born in different periods in different parts of the world. Oscillating between the US and Canadian border, 47-year-old James still struggles to get individuals to understand his true, talented self. Ten-year-old Ndumi on the other hand has recently started to thrive with the use of the letterboard. As he comes of age in Gauteng, South Africa, he notices that a lot of the world won't treat those of his race and neurotype with kindness, as James has experienced for most of his life, especially with law enforcement. To be a Black autistic male means that one's sense of childhood is cut short, and the need to be hyper-aware of your sur-roundings to avoid violence and abuse is frequent. Understanding and empathizing with individuals like Ndumi and James can widen communication and ultimately uplift respective societies for all races, genders, and neurotypes throughout the complex rhythm of our times.

Ujima
East Amherst, New York, USA

"So Kala, you read just two books this marking period?" one of my high school English teachers asked me, glaring.

"Yes," I replied while looking down and crafting a poem for my cre-ative writing class.

"Good luck in life. 'Scholar' athlete." The other students giggled, and I shrugged, pretending to appear unbothered. After class, I went to eat lunch and check Twitter in the bathroom quickly before re-treating to our school's library. Since I gave up on eating at the cafeteria shortly after beginning high school, and since we weren't allowed to eat in the library, I spent most of my two free periods journaling in the library.

Sure, it probably would've made significantly more sense had I actually studied at the library, but journaling and pretending to read while people-watching was much more fun. Occasionally, I was accompanied by one of my two library buddies who socialized like normal humans in the cafeteria before spending their second free period working on homework. One favored math and the other English, subjects that I had permanently abandoned and temporarily resented respectively.

Naturally, the English friend was more observant, and we often corroborated each other's fears of being hated and excluded. In literature, boys, and high school drama, she looked beyond the exterior and became fascinated by the subtle meaning beyond the surface. Math buddy, on the other hand, was more logical, albeit more sage as well. She was in the grade ahead of us after all. She would glide through her trigonometry homework and SAT prep while making fun of my "year-behind" woes that I had fact-checked from an English friend the day before. She was too big for our little library and the drama it overheard, and I both admired and envied her privilege to not pay attention to it.

One day, English library buddy asked me why I always just pretended to read the required books. Annoyed that she saw through my facade, I shrugged and told her that I read the summaries online out of spite. She laughed before proceeding to tell me about another girl who was looking at her funny at lunch—of which I would conclude with her that she's after the same boy that English library buddy likes, of course. Sitting in the last row of the section of two-person desk tables, English library buddy was none the wiser that I simply didn't like English, but I was bored of it. That year we primarily read Shakespeare and other British literature and early American literature. As one of the few Black kids at my school, I was tired of reading the same stories of those who I couldn't connect with. The overwhelming majority of the British and American historical literature we read was about white individuals. Unfortunately for me, the reading didn't help me connect well with my modern-day white peers in my classes. These modern-day kids at least listed each of their interests and favorite subjects, music, and everything else on social media. I didn't care to decipher the same cryptic "looking at me funny's" written as if it came straight out of the King James Bible that I found in my assigned reading.

As white girls in suburbia, I didn't expect either library buddy to care about or understand my annoyance with the predominantly white reading material. At the time, I decided to log my Black girl woes and write contemporary stories of Black people in my notebooks, keeping my desire to learn more about people like me hidden. However, I realize years later that it was a mistake to assume that my buddies wouldn't have empathized with me. The truth was that my library buddies were similar to me in that they enjoyed reading about *their* history and *their* modern-day stories, the only difference was that it was available to them. Had I been given more reading materials about Black people apart from slavery and Martin Luther King, I would have been more than content too. That is until I met an Asian American library buddy who did not see her culture in our readings. Or a gay library buddy. Or a disabled one.

As a Black girl growing up in suburbia, it took me an embarrassingly long time to understand the struggles that my Black counterparts faced with the police. Sure, security followed me in the stores as I browsed hair products and makeup, but I had never had armed police stop me because of my presentation alone. As the Black Lives Matter movement unfolded as I came of age, I learned everything I could about the plight that many Black individuals faced just a few miles from me in inner-city Buffalo, a US–Canadian border city just like James' Detroit. As I grew older, I strived to learn about people who didn't resemble me, such as those of different sexual orientations, and immigrants from faraway countries. I resented not learning about these people when I was a teenager and wondered how many never had the chance to since becoming an adult.

During my library hide-out days, I resorted to creating stories that I would one day read. Fortunately for me, however, I learned that I didn't have to read the same stuffy books to be a reader, and started devouring novels and nonfiction books about all sorts of cultures and people.

The next chapter will feature an autistic and non-autistic individual thousands of miles away. While they share a similar complexion, their culture couldn't be more different as a result of their shared Black history of the transatlantic slave trade a couple of centuries ago. Afiniki and Jason both faced unprecedented circumstances in their environment and were jolted with the responsibility of advocating for the most vulnerable in their communities in an African and African American context. Jason had the courage that bathroom-eating me could have only dreamed at the time, and Afiniki had the audacity and tenacity to not leave anyone behind, just as I now hope for my English and Math library buddies today. As the Black community should lean on the Black autism community and vice versa, I wanted to showcase the parallel of two different lives with two different neurotypes in Jason and Afiniki, fighting for the betterment of their Black cultures yearning to reconnect.

As for my library buddies, I've seen them support awareness causes in their grown-up lives. While I've generally lost touch with both of them, I stay connected with former English library buddy on

Instagram, and former Math library buddy on LinkedIn (as the wise professional that she is). I noted former Math buddy's engagement on posts about the Black Lives Matter movement, and the occasional engagement that former English buddy gave on my posts on being autistic. I think about how much of the world opened up to the three of us after we immersed ourselves outside of our required reading material. How dangerous the world is for those who didn't choose how people perceive them as a threat. How many Westerners go about their lives ignorant of the plight of others, but would mock those who weren't interested to learn even more about their societal norms?

When I wrote the story of James, I thought about Math buddy's love for facts and reason. When I wrote about Ndumi, I reflected on English buddy's bright eyes and fascination for things she couldn't see. Ndumi doesn't know what his future holds, but those spreading awareness and advocacy will make it so his future is the best it can be. One where proper diversity training is in place for authority figures, and empathy and engagement for those different than us is the new societal norm. With the collective effort of every human, I believe it's possible to undo generations of abuse. With the voices of James and Ndumi, and all of our desire for change, I believe that there's an alternate future out there that allows for diverse various perspectives and considerations in a little library, consumed and provoked by those sitting at a desk table for two.

Chapter 3
Changing Environments

Jason
Buffalo, New York, USA

Jason Cathcart never expected to be a community activist during wartime. He was a childhood friend of mine. Or rather, the older brother of my childhood track and field teammate. When we met for this project, he discussed memories of being scrutinized by his family and friends for watching anime as a teen and young adult. We marveled at all the signs that we were autistic in hindsight, and discussed how neither of us were diagnosed until our mid-twenties.

While I ran with his brother and my other teammates on the out-side lanes of the track, Jason frolicked on his own in the artificial grass in the infield. One day, I noticed he stumbled and fell while performing a Tai Chi routine on the grass. My teammates chuckled briefly, and I looked away. I was ashamed to look at someone acting weird and being alone, or rather free. At the time, I was ashamed to look at someone with a similar neurotype of myself but unmasked. However, it intrigued me that he didn't seem to mind who noticed, and he certainly didn't care whether we scoffed or looked the other way.

I wanted to know the man behind the anime-loving, brother-of-my-former-teammate. He told me all that I'd missed since moving away from home, most notably that he was academically dismissed from college at one point due to executive functioning challenges. He also joined an organization called DOPE Collective, a platform where he utilized his love for poetry and learning to help his community. Jason began attending many spoken word poetry sessions for the Buffalo community. On a snowy winter evening, you'd find him and several Black and Brown individuals in a bar on Bailey Avenue, snapping and reflecting the night away to the baritone of poetry.

We scheduled our next catch-up to hear more about his challenges in school as well as updates about his upcoming events in DOPE Collective. We had a three-week gap in between meetings. During that gap, the world watched in horror as a white nationalist terrorist targeted a grocery store in our hometown, leaving ten souls dead and another three injured. I remotely watched Jason and the rest of my hometown pick up the pieces of our community, and advocate for the right to protection and safety of Black people in Buffalo and around the world.

Afiniki
Maiduguri, Borno State, Nigeria

There was a bit of religious tension in Maiduguri, Nigeria in 2008. Usually, the conflicts dissipated after a couple days, weeks tops. Understandably, Afiniki Mangzha didn't expect the tension to ever be different. Meanwhile, she jumped for joy when she was informed that her volunteer internship was going to be converted to a full-time job upon graduation from university. In the midst of the 2008 global recession, and in a rural, low-income state of Nigeria called Borno, she felt more than fortunate to secure a job quickly right in her hometown. As a Christian, Afiniki felt her values were aligned with the Integrated Women and Youth Empowerment Center to help uplift the marginalized in Maiduguri. In this relatively peaceful region, Afiniki thrived in working with low-income women and envisioned a steady rise to an executive level in the organization.

In late 2008, the word "Boko Haram" started to grow from sparse whispers to rushed mutterings among the community. By the year 2009, the terrorist organization grew. Several men and boys began to disappear to fight for or against the terrorists, and women and girls started to be kidnapped quickly thereafter. Afiniki, a member of a religious minority in a now Islamic extremist region of the country, found herself situated at the forefront of providing a sense of refuge and restoration for her hometown. Frightened, Afiniki saw millions of individuals, some she knew and loved, flee for their lives and leave the state and region of the country. She witnessed survivors of terrorist attacks seek asylum elsewhere, and rejoiced when word came back that they were safe in their new home. In her region of the country, it was nearly impossible for women to excel in their career without the trials of terrorism. At the onset of Boko Haram, the religious extremists of Islam, Christianity, and other traditional religions would begin to not only make it difficult, but dangerous for her to thrive. She too could leave with the survivors. She knew there would be absolutely nothing wrong with that.

However, she recalled a quote in her favorite story in her favorite book: "perhaps you were made queen for such a time as this?" (*New Living Translation Bible*, 2021, Esther 4:14). Afiniki wasn't diagnosed with autism or another form of disability, but she saw several people with disabilities from her country pour into her city. In her part of the country, the term autism didn't exist, although Afiniki grew up with several autistic individuals in hindsight. Several of whom didn't breeze through university as she did. She wanted her friends and former colleagues who later self-diagnosed as autistic to be represented in her community. Like many advocates, neurotypical and neurodivergent alike, she wanted nothing more than to reduce harm and disparity in her environment.

Uncertain and startled at the sudden change and new meaning of her role in her new workplace, Afiniki scheduled her usual wake-up alarm, laid out her work clothes for the week, and prepared for the work week ahead.

A CALL TO ACTION

Jason
Buffalo, New York, USA

On Friday evening, Jason returned from his work in Buffalo, NY. He stopped by the local Tops supermarket, an oasis in a former food desert. He picked up a few groceries for the weekend, some frozen food and a couple bags of chips, in case his friends from DOPE Collective dropped by. By Saturday, he knew that his plans were canceled when the news reported a shooting at the Tops Supermarket.

He listened closer:

It was a mass shooting.

It was a hate crime.

It was a hate crime about race.

His race.

Events like these didn't occur in his city these days. Sure, there are gang-related shootings in certain parts of the city, but hardly mass shootings. Buffalo's a quiet city, with one of our common slogans on billboards on our highways reading "Keep Buffalo a Secret".

It couldn't happen in Buffalo.

Not at Tops.

It couldn't have been him.

Jason stayed glued to the TV in his apartment as the local WIVB Buffalo news channel acquired facts about the victims, the survivors, and the domestic terrorist. On the news, a survivor described that she tried to call 9-1-1 while in Tops. She had to whisper because the terrorist was nearby, to the 9-1-1 operators' chagrin. Annoyed that the victim was whispering, the operator hung up on her. That survivor had to then call her boyfriend to call the national hotline number (Kilpatrick, 2022).

What if the caller was disabled? Hard of hearing? Hard of speaking? Jason thought, *What if the caller had been me?*

Reflexively, Jason reached out to DOPE Collective. A community of creatives and activists, many of whom were autistic or neurodivergent like himself. He knew his community wouldn't want to sit still while the news escalated with doom. Generally, fundraising efforts serving the most marginalized in Buffalo were short-lived.

The lasting history of racist policy like redlining (the common practice of discriminating housing allocations by race or ethnicity) was
ignored among the benefactors, and actions were hardly taken.
This time, it was different. The people of Buffalo and the Western
New York community in general were in agreement that the terrorist was repulsive. The consensus was that the local community
members creating change are heroes, and they deserve funding.

According to their website, DOPE Collective aims to "foster rele-
vant, accessible, well-versed and sustainable learning tools while
demystifying institutional, colonial, and traditional practices." *How
can Buffalo be safer for the Black community living there? What
about other vulnerable demographics like the disabled and elderly?
What about those that are both Black and vulnerable?*

As Buffalo is a quiet city, Jason didn't immediately assume news
stations outside of local media would pick it up. That is, until Facebook asked to mark himself safe for his friends and family to see.
He flipped the channel, and it was trending nationally as well for
something other than its inches of yearly snowfall. On May 14th,
Buffalo was no longer a secret, and, in front of the world, our
hometown needed to combat hate by living up to its other slogan
of being Buffalo Strong.

Afiniki
Maiduguri, Borno State, Nigeria

At first, dozens of displaced people arrived in Maiduguri, Nigeria. As
the Boko Haram Insurgency increased, those dozens turned into
hundreds, and rapidly into thousands. Many of those that were
displaced due to their homes being overrun by terror were women
and children. Women fleeing were recently widowed, or with their

husbands missing for months. Children were arriving alone, unable to read, write or communicate about where they arrived from and where their parents were. Twenty-eight first languages are spoken in Borno State (reliefweb, 2017), so many of these displaced individuals were permanently unable to speak with the workers at the Integrated Women and Youth Empowerment Center.

"Even when we could understand, sometimes we don't even know the name of that particular community where the woman or child is from these days," Afiniki said. "They were just so, so alone." Afiniki's favorite book is the Bible. Her favorite book of the Bible is the book of Esther. She often uses that scripture as her motivation to help and protect her community in whatever way she can. Afiniki and her organization were funded by the Victims Support Fund, where she and her team provided over 6000 women with a micro-credit cash-scheme.

"It wasn't only that we just gave them money, and then collected it back later without any real change," she clarified, "A lot of the cash to women was used to acquire a new school, start a business, and save money to eventually be able to provide for their children and send them to school."

She recalled a disabled woman who learned how to make and package peanuts. She later began selling them as snacks and was able to feed herself and save money on top to reinvest in her business and in other disabled women like herself. In much of Borno State, autism isn't recognized other than as a general disability or a disease. With many of the women and children disabled with varying conditions, Afiniki and her colleagues also created a special school for women with disabilities. Like most places in the world, women and children with disabilities were especially vulnerable to violence, and women to gender-based violence. Their primary teaching outside of the state curriculum was around domestic violence; how to protect themselves, report it, and respond to it.

In the Book of Esther, Esther went against her culture of the time to stand up for and ultimately protect her people from death. In a world otherwise divided, Afiniki stood firm and used her position to make sure the most vulnerable of her people had a chance to thrive in Maiduguri. Afiniki's community came from Muslim, Christian, and traditional religious backgrounds. She made sure that she and her colleagues reflected their diversity.

For Afiniki, fulfilling her career goals in this organization paled in comparison to living by the true meaning of her faith of doing unto others as she would have them do unto her (*New Living Translation Bible*, 2021, Luke 6:31; Matthew 7:12). Throughout her tenure, she served her community of various ethnic tribes, languages, and religious beliefs. As the years passed, Afiniki saw women and children of many backgrounds slowly begin to pick up the pieces to their changing environment.

"The feedback—it was amazing. It really has been amazing," she said, grinning as she talked.

THRIVING THROUGH CHANGE

Jason
Buffalo, New York, USA

In Buffalo, Jason didn't want to reinvent the wheel, but he wanted to utilize his knowledge and understanding of the Buffalo community to put himself in the driver's seat for others looking to fund from outside Western New York.

He and his co-founders created a resource page of local and reputable food initiatives serving Buffalo. The Tops Grocery store was built in a former food desert. After the shooting, there were many opinions and proposals of what to do with the store; some saying they want to keep the store as a memorial, others saying they want to tear it down. Yet still, another segment wants to take a stand and reopen the store, in order to make a statement that terrorists won't stifle the community. After the shooting, however, the community needed a new oasis, and Jason provided bystanders and onlookers with just that.

He linked resources to several food banks, including those specifically for disabled individuals such as the "Home-Delivered Meals for Homebound Older Adults (60+) and People Living with Disabilities" initiative. He highlighted local free rides services for those living in Buffalo's zip codes that are most impacted, such as a religious organization called Hearts & Hands: Faith in Action. Also on the list were local overdose prevention services, and of course several mental health resources, including "Coaching for the Culture" located on Harlem Road.

"We used to be Harlem," he said, eyes drowsy yet resolute. "Jefferson Avenue [the street of the terrorist attack] used to be Harlem too." Jason was referring to the rich history of the Buffalo-Niagara area, from being a key location in the underground railroad that led some enslaved individuals to freedom in Canada, to being one of the nation's beacons of Black artists and creatives. In the 1900s, for example, the legendary W.E.B. Du Bois and several other leading activists, writers, and others initiated the group called "The Niagara Movement." These intellectuals met in Buffalo and at Erie Beach, Canada, the border to Canada being a mere four miles from Jefferson Avenue in Buffalo. A fact that those from Buffalo take pride in was that the Niagara Movement later became the framework for the National Association for the Advancement of Colored People, otherwise known as the NAACP (Allman-Badwin, 2014).

Given the history, Buffalo's Black community was no stranger to terrorism, like the KKK for example (Kowalski, 1972). Like our ancestors before us, it was time Jason assisted in rebuilding the Harlem of Western New York. He made it his priority to focus on love and the community, rather than hate. He advocated for those most vulnerable that were often overlooked. Not too bad for a man who got snickered at for watching anime and practicing Tai Chi.

Afiniki
Maiduguri, Borno State, Nigeria

Throughout the years, Afiniki climbed the corporate ladder to program manager in Borno State, Nigeria, where she maintained and assessed the achievements across the region. At one point, she realized that in nearly 20 offices across the region, there was not one person with a disability working there. With an increasing number of disabled displaced individuals seeking assistance from the Integrated Women and Youth Empowerment Center, she knew they needed to be represented. She and her team drafted several policies to make sure they are well represented in all offices across the region.

Additionally, Afiniki works with another Madiguri native, Zainab

Titus, on maintaining a literacy initiative that includes several books and educational materials in a mobile truck. Zainab and Afiniki received grants to empower young girls in their center to stay in school, like the coding initiative sponsored by Imperial College London. Afiniki embodied a powerful initiative to fight against the insurgency of hate and attack on the innocent people of her state. She and her team at the Integrated Women and Youth Empowerment Center continue to move, like Esther, in assisting the vulnerable to thrive, and protecting the freedom of religious expression.

THE ONLY CONSTANT THERE IS

Afiniki
Maiduguri, Borno State, Nigeria

Afiniki had been speaking to me on a tree stump in front of a green, breezy open space. There was no noise in the background other than chirping birds, and the only thing to disrupt us was the occasional network delay. She was recently given the responsibility of an executive role in the organization—a role that she dreamed of before the Boko Haram Insurgency.

In a world full of ongoing division and hate, those that advocate for the well-being of their communities and their freedom to thrive, while at the same time looking out for and listening to the most vulnerable will be those that succeed in the end. From disability assistance to terror, the world has a long way to go in advocating for the Black community, much less the autistic Black community. The only way forward is to keep being present, speak up, and shine a light of peace on the only constant that is change.

Jason
Buffalo, New York, USA

With all the advocacy on his organization's page and personal social media page, I finally asked Jason how he was doing psychologically. "You know, some days are good days, some days are not good days," he said. "Being with people helps you process this in a positive way." While on video, he started walking down the hallway in his apartment. He mentioned that one of his friends from DOPE Collective was over this time with some others, over to drink and eat.

"Just because this terrible event happened doesn't mean I'm going to stop living." Music and loud conversation echoed in the background as Jason walked from the living room couch to the dining table. For Jason, being among his community at DOPE Collective has helped him get through the tragedy. He and his group discussed the sentiment that it's okay to grieve, that it's normal to feel the need to slow down and reflect.

Unfortunately, there wasn't much time to do so when you zoom out to other national news headlines. The day after the tragedy in Buffalo, another mass shooting happened in a predominantly Asian church in California (NBC News, 2022). Shortly after that, another one occurred in Uvalde, Texas, killing 19 9–11-year-old students and two teachers. Of course, these were the shootings that have made the national news. As of July 5th of 2022, more than 300 mass shootings had occurred in 2022, killing 343 and injuring 1391 (Ledur, Rabinowitz, & Galocha, 2022).

Jason walked back to the couch, motioning to his friends that he'd rejoin them soon. "For me," he said, regarding grieving through tragedy, "the most important lesson I've learned was to take a step back and have my own time." He gave a relaxed smile as he talked about how he recently utilized most of his me-time sleeping in and napping. However, his smile faded as he spoke about his plans to travel to Philadelphia for a vacation. He shook his head, and his friends' commotion in the background softened in remembrance. Jason read on the news that there was a mass shooting in Philadelphia the night before he was supposed to leave. Exhausted, he decided to have a stay-cation at home instead, in his changing Harlem.

Ujima
Buffalo, New York, USA

Throughout my teenage years, track and field saved my life. When I moved from Japan to our town outside of Buffalo, New York, I was hit with what was later to be discovered as undiagnosed depression and anxiety. In middle school, I changed friend groups as much as I would change outfits, in a desperate attempt to find at least a few kids who wouldn't uninvite me from events. In high school during the day, of course, I kept to myself in my makeshift cafeteria-bathroom, and talked to very few people outside of English Library Buddy, Math Library Buddy, and my teammates.

For a long time, I saw track and field as my ticket out of my immediate surroundings. I was placed on high school varsity from the 7th grade, and won the High School New York State Championship titles from 8th grade. For me, it was my alter ego, because while many in my town saw me as the awkward girl who was not worth getting to know, the athletes and reporters of the region, state and soon to be country thought otherwise.

Before I knew it, I was invited to represent the United States on a relay team in a track meet in Jamaica. The same meet where we met Usain Bolt, and where two of my relay teammates would go on to later become Olympians. My athletic success was where I encountered minor irony when my worlds did collide.

My biggest joy from running for all those years was the kind of people I was able to be exposed to because of it. While I had a love–hate relationship with a lot of my high school peers, they ultimately reflected our sheltered suburban town. Where many of them scoffed at the "ghetto" black inner-city counterparts, and admired themselves for the lives our parents were able to provide us on the backs of systematic, generational racism and oppression. A lot of these conversations happened right in front of me, but I'm forever grateful I had the opportunity and empathy to see past their ignorance.

As an elite sprinter, I had the chance to be close to several other Black athletes from various parts of the United States. Apart from the US team in Jamaica, I was involved with other track teams with members from other high schools. In the summer, I was involved with a track club that funneled the best runners from across the Western New York region to compete at the state and national level. It was there where I met Jason's brother, and eventually Jason. I learned from running with athletes apart from my socioeconomic background that many individuals had more than track and school to worry about when they were home. Just because someone was winning races, and seemed popular, didn't mean that they didn't have to deal with the death of their teenage classmates from gun violence, or the disproportional rates of classmates and family having fatal drug overdoses. At the time, I was surprised to see so many differences in the environments my fellow Black athletes lived in.

It was during these supplementary training programs that I got to know not only fellow African American runners, but also African immigrants. In the year I won a national championship, a competitor from Wisconsin approached me to tell me how much she'd been following my success in track and was excited to meet me. We quickly exchanged social media profiles, and have since become lifelong friends. The woman is a second-generation Nigerian immigrant, who loved explaining and sharing her culture that stemmed from both the midwest in the USA and her ethnic group in Nigeria. It was from my track and field experience during my teenage years that I learned that there are so many different ways to be Black. Understanding that we all see and experience the world differently helped me to better understand and relate with those both within and outside my race for the years to come.

These days, when I overhear a conversation about an Olympian in my group of mostly academics, entrepreneurs, autism advocates, and/or writers, most people listening vehemently disbelieve me when I tell them that I not only know that Olympian, but competed with them. For the most part, I leave their disbelief alone and choose not to prove anything. For me, it only validates the stereotypes I had to overcome for anyone to understand that I was struggling, or that I was autistic. If autism advocates and researchers in today's world can't understand that I could be an elite athlete and autistic girl with depression at the same time, then how could my coaches? My teachers? My parents all those years ago? It made me feel more compassionate toward myself when I finally thought, how could I have known either?

It was for that reason why I later began to give students grace for not immediately connecting to someone like myself or Jason. Why I began to show professional grace for not immediately understanding someone with Afiniki's circumstance despite her ambitious smile and beautiful background scenery. Now that I'm a bit older, I have started to think about the kind of people I want my own hypothetical children to be exposed to, and the type of character I would want them to cultivate under my care and guidance. In the next section, Jude and Dr. T, an autistic father and mother respectively, are well known on social media for showcasing a term called intersectionality.

Intersectionality is about recognizing the necessity to acknowledge everything about an identity that marginalizes a person—being a Black autistic woman in a warzone, for example. Both Dr. T and Jude take the beauty and culture of what they know, and apply it to a world that may not necessarily understand them or the term intersectionality. I'm proud to be on their team.

Chapter 4

Parents Who Want Few Barriers for Their Children

North Carolina, USA • Chattanooga, Tennessee, USA

Dr. T
North Carolina, USA

Dr. T looked to the side. Her eyes seemed to grow incomprehensibly heavier as she counted on her fingers, one by one, the reasons why her young adult niece had had the police called on her.

"So, we have, for not looking as 'properly groomed' as proper ladies."

One finger.

"Probably because I had to sneak her into my office so she could get work done outside of her own open office floor plan arrangement... which apparently means she doesn't show up."

Two fingers.

"For stimming."

73

Three fingers.

"The police ultimately came when she experienced a meltdown where I'm sure she self-soothed by lightly hitting her head on a nearby wall in her room…Oh and her ex-friends were afraid she could harm herself."

Exasperated, Dr. T flung out both of her hands. She spoke about the delicate dance she has had to perform following the guardian advice of [predominantly white] fellow psychiatrists, and [predominantly silenced] cultural reality of many people of color. She's learned to do so all while picking and choosing what to model from her own family, who didn't realize autism could be in their lineage until her niece was diagnosed with it two decades later. In a way, her family, both well-meaningly and unwittingly, suppressed any disability or condition that could make life harder for an African American offspring, going back generations.

"You always have to ask yourself," Dr. T said, "Am I doing the best I can, or the best of what I know?"

Dr. T grew up in a small town in New York State as the youngest child of Georgian parents: her big-city mother and rural Georgian father. Now in her fifties, Dr. T took elements of her parental figures when caring for the upcoming youth of both blood and bond. Her father had a bachelor's degree from a Historically Black College or University (HBCU) in a stem field, a rare feat for a rural Black child in the segregated South. In Georgia, and as a young man who wasn't able to attend the same schools or use the same bathroom as his white counterparts, Dr. T's father struggled to find a job at the local factory despite his advanced qualifications. One day, he eventually received a call to work in upstate New York, and he left, transforming the lives of his family and descendants with the move.

Dr. T, on the other hand, excelled in the classroom by doing what she was told to do, nothing less, but often more. Dr. T often heard from her parents that times were changing and that she and her siblings needed to do their best in school for them to have the best life. A generation past Jim Crow, Dr. T's parents wanted to provide their children with everything needed for their children to accomplish their dream, so that their children's success could be greater than theirs. Still, Dr. T's parents made an effort to keep her and her siblings connected with the Black community at large, an effort that the community widely dropped by the time her niece entered the world.

The parents of Dr. T joined a movement called the Great Migration, which is described as the movement of millions of African Americans migrating from the Southern United States to the Northern United States in the era of severe racial violence and discrimination, particularly in the former slave states. Dr. T spoke about how any kind of illness or condition—even relatively common physical conditions that her parents had, was often hushed up and never spoken about. "If someone were to have a condition such as autism at the time, it would definitely have been buried when discussing with their children like me," Dr. T said. "Even if someone were to find out that someone was autistic for example...[white people] might take their job away, or you might not get that promotion, things like that. You didn't want to give [hiring managers] an even greater excuse to exclude you besides racism." She elaborated that such conditions would be silenced even among Black individuals outside the immediate family, as it could ostracize them among a budding migrant community that was forming in the north. Dr. T noted that her niece's suicide attempt during college was kept private, as her grandparents and Dr. T's parents chose to not tip off curious observers asking about her health. While her niece's immediate family felt more comfortable vaguely revealing that she was sick in general, Dr. T understands that there were cultural differences that deterred her parents from talking about their granddaughter's health apart from general respect for privacy.

Dr. T enjoyed her time in her second-generation migrant community of other suburban Black kids in New York State. During the peak of the Black Lives Matter Movement in 2020, she remembers that several work colleagues discovered for the first time hubs with names like "Hansel and Gretel" and "Jack and Jill." Dr. T was proud of how she was able to live as she called it "double lives" by being one of the few African Americans in her town during the week, then going to the nearest city to meet other Black individuals to maintain and preserve their culture. "So many were surprised how I and others would be doing all the school stuff. And then most weekends I would hang out with Black people from everywhere," Dr. T said.

Still, Dr. T discovered in hindsight that a condition that she struggled with all of her life wasn't looked into when she was in graduate school. She soared through school and university by working harder than everyone else. She struggled to keep up in medical school among fast readers, but she made up for it when she entered her clinical rounds in the later years of the program. Pushing through the pain and doing what she was told eventually earned her a spot in residency back in the south at Duke University. It was there that she was later diagnosed with a reading disability.

Nearly 25 years later, when Dr. T's adult niece also moved to North

Carolina, Dr. T remembers being concerned with her mental health conditions. As someone who specialized in psychiatry, she did the best she could to help her niece as she struggled to maintain relationships in that season. After the wellness check, and shortly after a second suicide attempt, Dr. T noticed herself feeling both relieved and concerned to learn that her niece was eventually diagnosed with autism spectrum disorder.

Like most guardians and like her parents before her, Dr. T didn't want her niece to have a life that was more difficult than it had to be. Even though times were getting better for both her and her parents' generation, Dr. T was saddened to see another barrier added to her niece's life in addition to being a Black woman in America. The psychiatry field as a whole also wasn't much help, generally describing the condition as a tragedy that negatively affected families. Still, Dr. T had to remember that her niece was still the person she was well before they all understood the condition. She remembered how she felt when she learned about her condition, and how she was ashamed of how it affected her career. And then, ultimately, feeling she let her parents down.

Dr. T was grateful for everything the generation before her did for herself and their descendants like her niece. In times of extreme stigma for their race, it was impossible to make allowance for any other condition like a reading disability or autism. Dr. T decided that it was up to her and her generation to confront such conditions head on with grace and calm. She lets her niece, now with an advanced degree like her, stim whenever she needs to, and take a break from open floor plans when she has to. And, when the time is right, she reminds her of their lineage who were resilient through unprecedented times such as 19th-century slavery and, in the 20th-century, Jim Crow and great migration.

Jude
Chattanooga, Tennessee, USA

In Chattanooga, TN, Jude looked straight ahead. He held each finger in the air, one by one as he described all the ways the doctors refused to believe that he or his children are autistic.

"I can't be autistic because I held a job before."

One finger.

"Because I was married."

Two fingers.

"Because I lost weight, I work out, et cetera et cetera."

He waved his hands, "And don't get me started on my children."

Jude realized that he was autistic after his oldest was diagnosed with attention deficit hyperactivity disorder (ADHD). His oldest often revealed to their dad and Jude's ex-wife that they were having trouble fitting in at school. Through Jude's advocacy, his oldest was eventually tested for autism, but the psychiatrist said they were on the threshold. At their school, the other Black students made an effort to protect Jude's child from bullying from the other students, although they didn't make much of an effort to be friends with Jude's child.

Observing the behavior of Jude's child with the other Black students, the teacher said that the child has plenty of friends when asked by the autism assessor.

"The [other students] knew them, but my child didn't know them at all," Jude said.

Jude, a transgender man, said his father is a Nigerian immigrant who utilizes his Ph.D. to teach as a professor. Jude describes how interconnected their Nigerian culture is, and the conflicts he and the rest of his family had to face when they moved to a predominantly white town with very few immigrants. Jude noted how his dad felt othered when he was the only one who beat his children like himself. Or how Jude's dad didn't approve of him marrying his wife as a lesbian. Or how he didn't approve of Jude divorcing his wife and later coming out as transgender.

Jude's parents were part of what is considered an ongoing Nigerian movement termed "Japa". Japa is a slang pidgin word that refers to the mass exodus of Nigerians leaving for better security, stability, and financial prospects. With an unemployment rate that is one of the highest in the world, many educated Nigerians are moving abroad in order to make better use of their degrees, to obtain advanced degrees or grow their careers abroad. Like Dr. T spoke about the great migration for African Americans a generation or two before, Nigerian immigrants like Jude's parents made an effort to maintain their culture and community in a similar hub in Tennessee. As Black people, like Dr. T, most wanted to keep conditions such as being autistic hidden. Already oppressed, parents reflexively wanted to have as few barriers for their children as possible. Because his parents did not accept Jude for who he was, his children missed out on growing up in their own Nigerian cultural hub as Dr. T had as a child. Jude had and continues to struggle with discovering his own definition of community apart from what he knew.

Jude felt himself drift further and further away from his upbringing and was determined to start afresh with a new communication style of openness. Seeing his oldest start to drift further from their new community, he decided his new style was going to begin by homeschooling them.

Hair slicked back, Jude continued to look straight ahead while he informed me of how he reached his breaking point with his child in the school system. "In their previous school, [the administration] would only give them like 15 minutes to eat meals because of COVID. They became very thin and lost weight," he said, looking down briefly before adding, "They take stimulants for ADHD and emotional regulation. But they cannot get a proper dosage if they're underweight." Jude described how he himself struggled with obsessive compulsive disorder (OCD)-induced eating disorders, stimming from gender dysphoria, followed by the stigmatization of being out as transgender. Not wanting his child to undergo a similar fate that was catalyzed by the pandemic, he decided to put his principles of openness into action throughout his child's full day.

Discussing his father's growing feelings of isolation when Jude was a teenager, he said, "Things came at him in waves." Back then, that led to Jude himself feeling isolated. Fast forward to the pandemic, Jude remarked, "And his profession, they thought Covid-19 came in waves too. So it was time to take my child out." Jude felt that the "waves" of the pandemic were leading his children to feelings of isolation and not belonging. He felt that he needed to make a change.

"It's been great to go at their pace..." he said, "if they're hungry, tired, anything. We're not in this confined deadline system. We both had to heal and realize that it wasn't me, that was harming my child. It wasn't my child. It wasn't even the teachers. It was the system not set up for them to succeed."

Jude describes how homeschooling has been amazing, but also lonely. At present, he and his child have gone on this journey for almost one year. At the end of the day, however, he has no regrets on taking a much-needed step out of a generational cycle of otherness.

"Things that I needed as a child, is what I needed to provide for my kids," Jude says, regarding breaking the cycle. "My child could trigger me. They have my face. But that's on me, not them."

Jude's youngest child later came into the room crying. Jude immediately paused our session to console them.

"Are you okay, honey?

Okay, good. I'm doing something that can help people.

I can help you with the batteries after my session, just give me some time, is that okay?

Thank you, do you need a hug?"

Jude described to me that his youngest needed help with the Xbox, but they were both able to agree that it could wait until after their meeting. Breaking back into his stoic behavior of looking straight ahead, he described what he hoped his children will grow up to have. What all of us need.

"I'm teaching them to navigate this world, when they don't deserve this world. They need a community where they no longer fear harm and otherness... We all deserve so much more. I want to parent them in a way [for them to know] that they do not deserve the conditions and circumstances they were born into. It is no one's fault, but we as a community need to do this together."

No more otherness, only togetherness—both Dr. T and Jude's quest in being generational change makers.

Ujima
Oxford, Ohio, USA

When I was a teenager, I wanted nothing more than to move far away from New York State. I assumed I would no longer have to live a double life as a high school loner and NY track star. However, just like Jude and Dr. T discovered that where they were from followed them in their new families, I learned the same lesson when I enrolled at Miami University on a full athletic scholarship.

After long school days of studying conditions like autism spectrum disorder during psychology class, I mostly enjoyed practicing track drills with my teammates. For some reason, I made many assumptions about conditions like autism being a tragedy that affected only the lives of parents of young middle-class boys. During practice later that day, I wouldn't be surprised if I talked with my teammates about what I learned about autism and how it seemed like an impairment that needed to be fixed. It would take years for me to understand that the thought process of and teaching methods for burgeoning academics like me were a part of the problem that affected families like Jude's and Dr. T's.

To add to the irony, I learned that I could no longer conceal my social awkwardness while living and studying with my teammates, like I thought I had among track people outside of my high school in Buffalo. In the common bathroom shared with the 30 girls (mostly athletes) on our dorm floor, I often overheard conversations about "going out." Flopping back to my dorm room with my flip-flops and a shower caddy, I'd eventually enquire with some of my teammates if they had any plans.

"Nope," they'd often say, before later leaving to hang out in another dorm room. I wasn't swift enough to gather my things to leave with them, but, to be honest, I needed the quiet time by myself to rejuvenate and study. With the help of social media, I'd later discover that they got dressed and left for a party from that other dorm room. In hindsight, I realized I didn't understand myself any more than they did, which made it difficult for many of my teammates to understand how to reach out to me. Regardless, I felt duped for happily studying in my quiet room for all of those hours.

A couple of my teammates hosted Bible studies in the dorm building across from mine. Sensing that I wasn't interacting with my peers, they invited me to join the group that they hosted specifically for freshmen. Interested in continuing the familiarity of growing up in church, and thrilled to be invited to anything, I happily accepted.

Sitting on the foot of a bottom bunk on one of the girls' beds, I nodded along as we read a familiar passage of the gospel. It was nearly impossible to stop myself from rolling my eyes at the other freshmen who commented on the passages and relating them to their lives at Miami that involved rushing sororities or finding the right extra-curricular. In the athlete space, we called non-athletes "nonners" and spoke about them as if we were military people speaking about civilians. I'm ashamed to admit that hearing a girl named Allyson speak about her roommate who was rude to her at first felt beneath me. Her long brown hair and the way she held herself reminded me of some of the girls in my high school who made me decide to eat my lunch in the bathroom.

"My roommates are my teammates, and we have a lot of other things to worry about other than interpersonal group drama," I lied, well, at least to myself. My older group leader teammates raised their eyebrows at me, making me nervous that they would shame me for being an outcast from the world of campus athletes in front of a bunch of "nonners."

"Cool," Allyson innocently said instead, "then where are they?"

I got along with athletes around New York State relatively well as a highschooler, so I assumed that my only chance of having friends again would be among fellow athletes. Around campus, it was clear that most of the athletes hung out amongst themselves, with a few other Black students joining in with the Black athletes. For me, what worked for the previous few years of my life seemed like my only chance at friendships. However, as Dr. T and Jude would say, I didn't have to repeat history. Fortunately for me, being isolated from the social scene provided me the chance to study more than anyone I knew. I became passionate about psychology and took steps to solidify research opportunities and my chance at achieving a neuroscience co-major. Before I knew it, my passive interest in a lifetime of track drifted towards an active desire to understand more about people, their data and making sense of it all.

"They're not here," I confessed to Allyson at Bible study, my first of many times saying that phrase in my time on campus.

One year later, I became more immersed in obtaining a neuroscience co-major, and enrolled in cell biology. I'm now horrified at how quickly I became more fascinated at learning the biology behind "tragic" conditions like autism in order to be part of the work that could solve it. Passion wasn't ever enough to drive me, though. I knew that I needed to study significantly more than anyone I knew in order to achieve a decent grade, but that cell biology class specifically was whooping me. In that classroom, I, at first, sat in the back where those around me were often scolded for talking and giggling. After a couple of classes, I recognized the long brown hair in the front middle of the class, rapidly taking notes. In a relatively full lecture hall, I realized that there were two empty seats next to her on both sides.

"Hey Allyson," I said, after abruptly leaving the one-sided conversation with the only other Black girl in the class as she recalled the shenanigans she, my teammates, and many others had last night without me. My guilt of feeling like I was too different from Allyson because I was an athlete, and judging her for what she looked like (nonBlack) nearly scared me away from walking down the stairs to join her near the front row. The irony of me stereotyping someone for what they looked like and being afraid of what happened in the past was not lost on me. In the back rows of the lecture hall, I decided I didn't want another person to feel "othered" or labeled like I did, so I decided to break the cycle of judgment.

"I'm so behind in this class, so I need to just listen and take notes," I said as I parked my large notebook next to Allyson's and sat to her left. I couldn't afford to start a conversation that may or may not make me feel as left out as the one a few rows back. She nodded and smiled reassuringly, and I remembered then her saying that she was a zoology major several months before, and loved her subject as much as I loved mine.

Now it was my turn to stop labeling and othering. At the end of the lecture, we smiled at both of our pages full of notes, and I assumed we'd part ways without a word. Instead, I took a deep breath and asked Allyson how the situation with her rude roommate ended in her freshman year.

Part 2
Progress

Chapter 5
Love, Autism, and Ramadan

Kouro-Maïram
Dakar, Senegal • Quebec, Canada

Kouro-Maïram wasn't that interested in dating. She was from a diverse, family-oriented background. She and her family moved often, changing homes in France, Saudi Arabia, Senegal, and Texas throughout her childhood. She loved the bond her family held in person, so she never considered dating someone long distance as her family kept moving. Plus, she had a strictly religious family. With a Muslim father from Mauritania and mother from Senegal who forbade PDA (public displays of affection) for their young daughter? No, Kouro-Maïram wasn't interested in dating. She couldn't have been.

That is, until she fell for a guy at a New Year's Celebration. Months later, she saw him once again during an annual holiday trip to Senegal. In this holiday time of reflection, community, and prayer, Kouro-Maïram was reminded to empathize with those less fortunate than her, and give to those in need. It was always hard for her to interact with people, especially in large groups. However, deep down, Kouro-Maïram wanted to share her inner self with someone outside of her family, and was especially keen to do so in a one-on-one setting. Throughout the celebration, Kouro-Maïram's feelings for this guy were as clear as the self-directed autism screener she later took. She then embarked on the first step of her journey: understanding and empathizing with others first started with understanding herself.

The scene: a New Year's celebration in the vibrant city of Dakar. Kouro-Maïram's family only comes to Dakar during New Year's and the secular Christian holiday season of Christmas. To this day, Kouro-Maïram doesn't like it when she and her family host large parties. The energy and preparation needed for it were above her threshold of tolerance. "It's hard to describe. I mean, I have to chat, entertain, play board games with cousins...and I love board games— and my cousins! But it's all very energy-consuming. Just because they're family doesn't mean I want to entertain them," Kouro-Maïram said, portraying the phenomena of being overstimulated in an environment like gatherings in places that were previously seen as a refuge—like her Senegalese home for example.

Kouro-Maïram also celebrates Eid with her family during the school year. Eid al-Fitr celebrates the end of the month-long fast during Ramadan, the second of the two times a year she was there. Money is provided to the poor and vulnerable during the time of Eid prayers, followed by supplication for Allah to provide forgiveness, mercy, and blessings for all living creatures across the world. Kouro-Maïram loved her religion and culture. However, the prayers, sermon, and supplication were also always followed by additional celebration and other energy-draining activities. It was complicated for her to partake in one and not the other, but, to her, it was worth it. The culture and religious substance that took place during Eid ultimately shaped how she grew to understand herself later in life.

Like most parties, the New Year's one in Senegal carried on anyway. Kouro-Maïram's winning streak at a board game with her cousins was placed on a long-term pause when she came across a family friend by chance. Loud music. Louder cousins. Cordial banter and joyous laughter. Not to mention all of her family present, and his as well. To Kouro-Maïram though, all of that was put aside temporarily. It was as if she and he were the only people at the event. What began as reaching for the same hors d'oeuvres, evolved into discussing their favorite food, and eventually segued to discussing everything else about each other.

"We met through serendipity," Kouro-Maïram said, and I smiled as I noted the similarity to the beloved 2000s Disney movie series *High School Musical*. A karaoke room, a catchy song, and a missing female singing partner were all that were needed to complete the serendipities.

"I mean, of all the NYE parties of Dakar, of all the girls at the party— though I must've been the only one with a 'fro—he approached me. And with nothing more than a simple 'hey' to start. We were both surprised that we were both English speakers at a primarily French-speaking party," Kouro-Maïram added.

Kouro-Maïram has an older sister and brother, and is sarcastic with her sister to the point where she used to be confronted for sounding rude. Her sister is a fun-spirited extrovert who loved Kouro-Maïram incredibly, and she shared a room with her sister until she was 14.

"I was SUFFOCATING!" Kouro-Maïram said. She described how her sister would kiss her cheek multiple times a day, all of which Kouro-Maïram would immediately and systematically rub off. It wasn't until a few years later that she realized it was a matter of the cognitive and energetic costs linked to her being autistic and introverted. Like many autistic and introverted individuals out there she realized she needed time to herself but grew up lacking it.

Eventually, disclosing her new boyfriend to her siblings a few days later was no different. She was asked many questions about her personal moral beliefs. Kouro-Maïram reflected on her views and decided to stop seeing him on her own. "I was raised with dating being forbidden and sinful, and I felt that my interest in him was in fact a sin," she said. However, their chemistry was "off-the-charts," and Kouro-Maïram wanted to keep getting to see him, empathize with him, and ultimately know him. After serious reflection of whether or not it felt sinful and wrong to her (plus the frequent help and encouragement from a couple of friends), she recontacted him, and their relationship began.

He was diagnosed with autism very early in life, and, for a while, Kouro-Maïram didn't think much of it. His mannerisms and behaviors were a lot like her brother, of whom there was a running suspicion that he might be on the spectrum. The social impairments and behaviors didn't resemble Kouro-Maïram on the outside, and no one expected her to be autistic too, not even herself. Or at least, not for a while.

Kiera Adams
University of Oxford, England

Two miles away from the psychology building, my former classmate and I reminisced about the stress and challenges that was our master's program at the University of Oxford during the height of the Covid-19 pandemic. Kiera Adams is now a D.Phil. or Ph.D. student at the University of Oxford where she broadly studies social cognition in autism. While Kiera Adams doesn't identify as either Black or autistic, her insight into her research is important. With the majority of autism researchers not looking like most individuals featured in this book, it is important to have ongoing discussions and collaboration with researchers and policymakers from all backgrounds.

Like myself and many others, Kiera Adams had unlearned a lot of ableist perspectives. For example, when she was an undergraduate student at Cambridge, she learned and conducted most of her research around the extreme-male-brain theory. This theory was designed by her previous research supervisor Simon Baron-Cohen, author of many high-profile autism articles. The theory posits that most autistic traits are related to male traits, for example preferring talking about dates and weather patterns as opposed to relationships (Baron-Cohen, 2002).

Of course, this theory is flawed in many ways, most notably being that males are not actually more likely to be autistic. However, males are currently more likely to be diagnosed with autism (Whitlock *et al.*, 2020). When even Baron-Cohen himself pivoted away from the theory, other researchers (and the rest of the world for that matter) took longer to see its flaws. Parents, teachers, and even aspiring researchers like Kiera were still under the impression that autism was primarily a male condition.

"I am grateful for my experience with him," Kiera Adams said regarding her time being mentored in his lab at Cambridge. "But I used to be very skeptical of [autism and genders] having such well-defined cognitive differences. I wondered if there were maybe different features about how autism manifested in girls and women. It's pretty clear that diagnostic criteria have been centered around males."

Kiera Adams and I discussed the importance of autism researchers like herself listening to the autistic community, including those that have intersectional identities, like being in the LGBTQ+ community or being a racial or ethnic minority.

"There's not much diversity in academia. The MMR vaccine ['vaccines cause autism'] scandal was a prime example (Gross, 2009)," Kiera Adams said, regarding how much authority and impact researchers can have even without being accurate or communicating with the autism community. "And I think I have even more of a responsibility to be mindful about not just how the research will look to other researchers, but also the autism community. The research community needs to listen to autistic women and girls, and not just study them." Kiera Adams and I paused to drink our tea while reflecting on the current state and progress of academia.

Kouro-Maïram
Dakar, Senegal • Quebec, Canada

Later, Kouro-Maïram relocated to France with her family. Despite coming from a tight-knit family, she and her boyfriend decided to remain long distance and continue to see each other on their annual family vacations to Senegal. She continued to do so when she moved to Quebec, Canada to enroll in undergraduate studies.

While reading more about her boyfriend's autistic characteristics, Kouro-Maïram stumbled upon an article about autism in women. "Then I took that famous checklist," she said, referring to a list of symptoms most noticeable in girls created by Samantha Craft

(2018) "...and was like 'oh my god, that's me!' My boyfriend said that if I didn't tell him I read the checklist that he would've assumed I was the one that wrote it, it was that perfect for me."

The low and late diagnosis rates in women and girls are often due to the high influx of information about autism that is specifically about boys and men (Werling & Geschwind, 2013). Like Kouro-Maïram, most girls read these symptoms, notice their autistic male friends, and regard it as being a completely different condition than theirs—if they were to think they had a condition at all.

Laughing, I told Kouro-Maïram how I also grew up around autistic people. How my track coach once pushed me out of the way to tend to my autistic male teammate, while those around me would shrug as I described symptoms of a meltdown or panic attack. How I studied psychology in undergrad, studied and aced exams relating to autism and neurodivergence with a straight face, and even had my brain scanned as a control sample in a lab experiment at my work that was studying autistic individuals at Massachusetts General Hospital. Like Kouro-Maïram, all I saw in the media were boys, mostly white boys when I was growing up, and never equated it to myself.

Kouro-Maïram is currently striving to become an autism researcher one day, and discussed her disregard for researchers who paved the path of misunderstanding in autism in girls. She recently spoke in a panel discussing her distaste about the Spectrum 10K study led by Baron-Cohen about finding genetic and environmental factors related to autism (Dattaro, 2022).

"Girls and women sometimes show different symptoms," Kouro-Maïram added, reading my mind. "We're socialized to hide our autistic traits or anything about us that's different or makes us

95

vulnerable. It's scolded out of us really quick. When I lived in France, I noticed that we were quite behind in autism, ADHD, and other neurodivergent conditions." From 16 years old, Kouro-Maïram saw a psychiatrist for several years when she lived in France. She rolled her eyes when she reflected on how she wasn't diagnosed with anything but ADHD, and that wasn't until right before she left at 18 after seeking out the diagnosis herself.

Kouro-Maïram continued to read books about autistic women. She had the privilege of knowing several languages, and reading the rare content in both French and English. Months later, with the encouragement and support from her boyfriend, Kouro-Maïram braced herself and decided to do what her boyfriend never had to do as an adult. What Kouro-Maïram's parents never could have done for her brother, and what her brother decided not to do for himself as an adult. Unsure, nervous, but also excited, Kouro-Maïram decided to have a formal autism assessment. She wanted to finally understand what she didn't see for the first 20 years of her life.

Kouro-Maïram came from a culture and society that had the added stigma of a condition like autism. Her parents were highly educated and excelled abroad, making her family very privileged in her community to help people in her home countries of Mauritania and Senegal. Kouro-Maïram described the societal pressure of being their children as "having no excuse to fail, and no reason to fail." Despite the potential social stigma that a diagnosis could label her as a failure, she pursued one to acquire more information about herself so that she could ultimately succeed.

That is, until she was temporarily stumped. It turned out that her area in Quebec didn't have an adult diagnosing center. Scratching her head and trying to remain unphased, she decided to look into her options. One option that she thought of was to go into the public sector, only to find out that the waitlist was very high.

"How high?" I asked, genuinely curious about the state of Canada's healthcare.

Kouro-Maïram shrugged, " Eh, I don't remember anymore."

"Weeks?"

Vigorous headshake, "More like months."

Impatient about the waitlist, Kouro-Maïram decided to go through Canada's private healthcare.

Scrolling through the internet, Kouro-Maïram was surprised and hopeful regarding the number of neuropsychologists in her area. She shortlisted those who specified that they were knowledgeable about assessing adult women with autism and booked an appointment from there. She tried not to faint at the cost of the assessment, racking up to $1900 for most kinds. Fortunately, she was able to continue to scroll to find an assessment option that didn't include an IQ test. She took a sigh of relief when she was able to reduce the cost to $1100, and counted her blessing that her family was able to assist her with the cost.

Kiera Adams
University of Oxford, England

As a researcher among the famous and scenic buildings at Oxford, England, Kiera Adams now studies conditions that are under-researched, such as interoception and eating disorders. She was published in the *Journal of European Eating Disorders Review* in 2022 (Adams *et al.*, 2022). She has made an active decision to research traits that are currently more symptomatic in women and girls, such as eating disorders presently being at a higher rate in this demographic (Hoek & Van Hoeken, 2003). Kiera Adams also proactively listens to my content and writing from a Black autistic woman's perspective.

"Once I started my Ph.D. at Professor Bird's lab, I began to appreciate his research methodology that didn't focus on a cause of autism," Kiera Adams said, after we briefly discussed the thin line between discovering a cause and eugenics. "Here [at my lab at Oxford] it's more on identifying areas that perhaps autistic people suffer disproportionately with, and identifying ways to manage that. So it's also very much escaping the narrative that autistic traits are an inherently bad thing, or something that needs to be managed, which I don't think is the case. It's looking at maladaptive behaviors that can co-occur more frequently, and discovering the best ways to heighten well-being for all."

Kiera Adams credits her experience, exposure, and friendships with autistic individuals from varying backgrounds for allowing her to see the duty she has to be an advocate for the autistic community. After listening to voices that are often silenced, she pivoted to supporting those voices more effectively. At present, Kiera Adams's research focuses primarily on eating disorders, a topic that will be further discussed later in this book.

Kouro-Maïram
Quebec, Canada

One month later, Kouro-Maïram was diagnosed with autism. She added that to her recent diagnoses of ADHD, language processing disorder, and dyscalculia.

"That's Math dyslexia," Kouro-Maïram added, when I asked her to spell it for me.

When she was next home for Eid, she decided not to tell her brother, she figured he wouldn't care to know if he didn't want to know about his own. Besides, they were so different from each other, she figured he wouldn't believe it. She told her mom, and after a bit of research and studying, as she does during her day job as a professor, she came to realize it made sense. She also told her sister, who was excited to learn more about it. Kouro-Maïram later reflected on her sister and other loved ones' understanding of her withdrawing from their extroversion. "That is precious and rare," she said, "and they did so without knowing of my diagnosis exactly, but because they knew and understood my intentions were never to make fun of them, degrade them, belittle them." Kouro-Maïram was inspired to give herself the same grace that those like her sister gave her.

As if figuring out her new diagnosis at university wasn't difficult enough, Kouro-Maïram and her boyfriend broke up amicably. Secretly, of course, as most of her family still didn't know about the relationship. While she was still establishing trust with her new university friends, she had to recover from the romantic loss on her own. To do that, she embraced the true power she gained from empathizing with and understanding her true self.

Two New Year celebrations passed in Senegal and two Eid observations came and went around the world. Her family hosted both sets of events, as usual. The music played, per tradition. In the first year during New Year's, Kouro-Maïram saw her secret boyfriend, and he high-fived her for the diagnosis, in person that time.

"One of us!" he said, and they laughed. They reminisced. They beamed, knowing that the attendants were none the wiser of their romance.

By the second New Year, he and Kouro-Maïram had already broken up in Canada a few months before the celebration. However, with her love and empathy she had for herself and others, she was able to be thankful to have him a part of her family's celebration—although she could do without the noise of some of the others.

Before the New Year countdown, her cousins were animated about a board game, per tradition. Kouro-Maïram looked at her ex to say goodbye again with her eyes. Instead, he joined her in taking a deep breath. Together, they gathered all the energy needed to make it through the chaotic event of her formerly favorite part of the event, hosted by her loving family in the center of their cherished culture. One more simultaneous breath was taken for good measure. Kouro-Maïram and her ex, now with an unsuspicious distance between them, headed toward her favorite cousins to join in on the board game.

The lack of research and representation of autistic women and girls is vast and (un)present world-wide. Kouro-Mairam, a world traveler, was an adult before she finally "saw" herself as an autistic woman. Young researchers, like Kiera Adams at the University of Oxford, are asking more questions about what it means to be autistic. The presence of emerging academics like Kiera Adams, working in

collaboration with aspiring researchers and outspoken representation of those like Kouro-Maïram, will allow autistic women and girls
to not only have better awareness about autism but also have better understanding of themselves.

Ujima
Oxford, Ohio, USA

Like Kouro-Maïram, I and many other Black autistic people also
had our share of cultural clashes and misunderstandings. Obviously,
Kouro-Maïram's occurred between her religion and various dynamics across the world. For me, it was primarily a clash between the
box I was placed in, and budding interests I wanted to pursue.

In college I felt that I was seen as hopelessly awkward, and woefully
one-dimensional. At the end of my sophomore year, after a few se-
mesters of trying to fit in, but before I reconnected with my friend
Allyson, I fell into severe depression while on the track team. For
me, the social utopia I wanted college to be was not my reality as I
continued to be excluded from activities both within and outside
of the athlete world. I tried to focus on my grades, but I gave up
when I looked around and felt that many in and outside of college
seemed to have put me in the "track star" box, and I felt like I could
never rebrand. I snapped after a poor grade on an exam and I went
to the nearest secluded trail to hike, cry, and say both sorry and
goodbye to my life. While on the trail, I saw a few snails, taking me
back to my childhood years in Okinawa. I frowned at the realiza-
tion that I had no desire to train myself to move forward, like how
I used to train snails long ago. I was spiraling, but I didn't know it. A
few days later, I attempted to end my life.

I want to put this next Ujima section in the form of a letter to
the current director of Disability Services, Stephanie Dawson.

Unfortunately, Stephanie took the role well after I graduated college, and I had no idea about the Disability Service department during my college years. The following letter will hopefully serve as one of hope for those in their college years, or parents with emerging young adults.

Dear Stephanie,

You didn't know me yet, but I would do anything to make it so you did. Many years ago, I was horrified to wake up in urgent care in the hospital, connected to an itchy sensory-nightmare IV.

I spent days at an inpatient hospital, knowing that I would eventually have to resume my old life as if nothing ever happened. I constantly wondered what was wrong with me. The doctors tried to help me understand, but I think we both knew the diagnosis of bipolar was most likely false. Looking back through the years, I often scan for ways I would have been able to walk past your department, and maybe recognize that I needed help not only with my mental health, but with regulating symptoms of a neurodivergent condition as well.

Unfortunately, I mostly stayed on the opposite end of campus when I was medically released from track while being able to keep my scholarship. I didn't quite make it to Disability Services, but I decided to pursue my interests and goals like any "nonner" student would do in college. My life changed when I was accepted and started working at a psychology lab on research on eating disorders and suicidality, as well as a behavioral neuroscience lab focusing on depression and anxiety. At the time, no one, including the doctors and myself, suspected I could have a neurodevelopmental condition such as autism. I went back to school with the same accommodations as before (none), but with the understanding that I had the rest of my life to better get to know myself.

I know in hindsight that the Disability Services is open for anyone to seek help in tutoring, mentoring, or other accommodations. I also now understand how my experience with others wasn't exclusively my fault or theirs. I simply needed more help and support, but at the time, my "track star" mask made it impossible for myself or others to understand. Years later, I was happy to hear you discuss how the department has been in better communication with other departments, including working with the Diversity Affairs department which supports minority students. I relish how you took the time to connect with the Alumni Affairs department, and later me as we strategized ways we could get other students the help and support that they need. As two Black women, I have loved how we have worked together to reach out to demographics that are more vulnerable to be misdiagnosed or undiagnosed with various disabilities at Miami. One year at a time…I'm confident and proud that Miami and other colleges in the United States are now raising more efforts to look out for students with differing needs than those in their immediate environment.

While no one in the research labs knew what I experienced, I found it cathartic to conduct individual research on a topic that I had experienced firsthand recently. It kept me grounded when I received pulls from my past to shrink into what I outgrew. My life without track was also busy. I had several meetings with Miami's athletic department reps to work for them during my research hours in order to retain my scholarship. I worked on my honors thesis that focused on characteristics of suicide as it pertained to student-athletes. I also enjoyed volunteering at the crisis hotline which allowed me to give back to those who had previously helped me. Not to mention, I was always invited to socialize with my colleagues in those endeavors. Over the course of the year and a half after my attempt, I slowly gained more empirical insight and understanding of how people in various ages, cultures, and life circumstances could come to a low point as I once had. I realized I was finally training myself like I did the snails years ago. It was a new life that no department could make me give up.

But here's where I needed you then, and where subsequent inter-departmental collaboration has been better now. When I refused to work for the athletic department during my research hours, and proposed times outside of standard working hours, some athletic department leaders said that it was more important for me to do what they said, and simply graduate late if I needed to conduct research later. I stood my ground and with the assistance of more rational athletic department leadership, I was able to retain both my passions and my scholarship, but not without being shaken up. But I was still confused on what was "so wrong with me." Not too long after that conversation, I experienced my first panic attack.

I know others aren't as lucky as me to have a friend like Allyson who came over at 3 am to help me cope and also gave me a blanket she had hand-knitted. I also was fortunate to have a psychiatrist to help me to learn to breathe through these situations—something I know Disability Services currently offers. I know that we're both excited for incoming cohorts of students and families who understand themselves and their needs better to seek out these accommodations. Most importantly, it is exciting to see how the department, and others around the country, are looking out for *students who may experience emotional hurdles for the first time on campus.*

I can't wait to hear more from you about how the department and ones on other campuses have made progress on preventing different kinds of students from spiraling like I did on that snail-ridden day on the trail.

Sincerely,
Kala Allen '16

Over the course of junior and senior year of college, through my special interests in psychological research and participation in several labs, I emerged from under my perceived brand of "track star" to the brand of "researcher". I was lucky that, because of my access to classes and labs, I did not stress over leaving the box that I was put into in the past. I know that others, like Kyron and Shangwe in my subsequent chapter, had similar hurdles and even harsher circumstances on the other side of the world. Thankfully, rebranding is a tool that they too could utilize from thousands of miles away.

Chapter 6
Translations for Autism

Kyron
London, England

"Put your fucking face down!" a Black police officer howled at Kyron. Frightened and upset, Kyron's hands began to shake as he struggled to be in touch with language or his own movement. In his borough in London, England, Kyron said he felt like he was experiencing a meltdown, in hindsight.

"I was 20 and had been living on my own at the time," he recalled. "The police made an assumption about me being a gang member because of where I was located and for my mannerisms. At the time when they approached me, they were undercover." He rolled his eyes when reflecting back on the incident. By this part of the interview, my fists were permanently clenched, leaving my transcription software to take all remaining notes. Kyron's British accent also needed my full attention to follow along. "But, I know my rights, and so I [eventually] questioned authority."

Kyron grew up among loving relatives, namely his mum, dad, grandparents, and two older siblings. Outside of family, however, he had a difficult upbringing with the school system prior to that moment. He was removed from three schools before finishing secondary school or high school. Kyron didn't blink when he spoke about how he was put on the most severe level of the Special Education Needs registry from the nursery, or from the time he was a baby.

In a primarily Black and poor environment, he was on the receiving end of underfunding and burnout of many that worked in his communities. A Black headteacher, who Kyron referred to as Miss Trunchbull from Matilda, tore one of his drawings he did for art class at the age of six.

"Right down the middle," Kyron said, adding that he left the class and ran out of school in distress. His mom later received a call that "he just left." A new note was subsequently added on his records for his mother to see that he had persistent disruptive behaviors. By nine, Kyron was kicked out of his first primary school, and by ten, his label upgraded to oppositional defiance disorder.

"They wanted to place me under the preschool-to-prison pipeline," Kyron said while shaking his head. In total, he received support for his disrupted behavior for seven years. He has no one to thank but himself, his mom, and God for his pipeline breaking before it was too late.

Shangwe
Moshi, Tanzania

Around the same time in rural Tanzania, Shangwe gave birth to her oldest son Daniel. In her already rocky marriage and tumultuous situation with in-laws, Shangwe held her son tight through emotional and physical abuse in their village. It didn't take long for Shangwe to realize that Daniel wasn't developing as a typical infant, toddler, and later child. For one, Daniel didn't speak, and he fidgeted more than his younger siblings Shangwe later bore. He also didn't understand spoken instructions in the way that she or the rest of her family did. Still, Shangwe's patience never wavered, but her already frustrated husband's did. The abuse and cheating escalated to the point where she and Daniel were banished from their own house. Her in-laws rejected her as well, as did the surrounding neighbors. In need of money to support herself and her son, Shangwe looked for work nearby and kept Daniel with a nanny.

"I felt so alone," Shangwe recalled, "but I at least had God and my son." I heard and briefly saw Daniel, now a teenager, play by shouting and waving his hands in the background of his mom's screen. I waved at Daniel while Shangwe shushed him with a smile.

Shangwe began to settle into her new life after a few weeks. Her son was happy when Shangwe returned home from work every day. However, Shangwe soon became worried after Daniel looked frightened as she was on her way out the door, as Daniel was eating his strict breakfast preference of tea and bread. It was a matter of days after her initial suspicions when Shangwe came home from work only to see Daniel badly scarred with burn marks.

"They wanted to make sure I suffer, so they poured boiling water on him," Shangwe told me, before showing me a horrifying picture of Daniel with burn marks on most of his back. With both of our eyes heavy and wet, I asked Shangwe to elaborate on what happened. She explained to me that their culture has a history of both witchcraft and Christianity. She and her neighbors identify as Christian and see witchcraft as evil. During her first few weeks in her new neighborhood, she knew that her neighbors and nanny were complaining about her son, particularly about his abrupt noises and mannerisms. "[The neighbors and nanny thought] that I engage in witchcraft and make sacrifices to the devil, which is why my child behaves like this..." Shangwe said. Scratching my head, I had to ask her to repeat herself, partially because of her thick accent as a non-native English speaker, but primarily because of the appalling nature of abuse on disabled children that I had not known occurred. While Kyron was mislabeled as being aggressive and a threat in England, Daniel was mislabeled as being the result of his mom's witchcraft in Tanzania. In environments dominated by white and Black individuals alike, stereotypes and cultural perceptions made it so an autism diagnosis—and the support that could accompany it—was lost in translation.

"Most people were not understanding," she added, citing a previous case where her neighbors and nanny attempted to burn Daniel. They proudly admitted this to Shangwe after she approached the nanny regarding his boiling water scars. Frustrated and alone, Shangwe took Daniel to various hospitals to find answers for both herself and those who tried to do her harm in her new area. "When [Daniel] was four, the doctors were not aware of the autism," she concluded in retrospect. At first Shangwe tried to send her son to the next nearby town for school. She gasped when the teacher sent a picture of another pupil after Shangwe insisted she see how he was doing. She quickly sent her brother to the school to check on Daniel as she had a court meeting for a divorce case. When the brother also confirmed that the original boy was not his nephew, and that Daniel was actually extremely thin and traumatized, they took him home immediately. It took him about two weeks for her son to get back to his diet, normal weight, and emotional stability since before he was placed in that school.

At a loss of how to stop the abuse, and with no respite in sight, Shangwe did what any loving mother would do and decided to move her son to a safer environment. She moved to a town called Moshi, a small upgrade from her previous rural neighborhood. When they unpacked, she decided there that she wasn't going to stop looking for answers about the source of Daniel's behaviors, and how she could support him in the best way that she could.

Kyron
London, England

Kyron was held on the floor by the police officer for nine minutes total in London. When he tried to report it, the court later felt that the violence on Kyron was needed for the intended outcome. Kyron described to me how he felt, for Black men with autistic traits like him, "early intervention, prevention and then criminalization is the intended outcome" rather than noticing him for the talented individual that he is.

"Apparently I have an issue about rules and routines," Kyron said, "[The police] came in plain clothes, didn't show IDs, grabbed me, didn't say a word, didn't say his name..." He sighed, "How can I not be oppositional when I'm attacked?" At 20 years old, Kyron was appalled at how the legal system worked for people like him.

To this day Kyron has never received an autism diagnosis, due to the barriers of access. He remembers how his mother was frequently told that Kyron had disruptive behavior from instances such as not sharing toys. During the hearing Kyron saw that the mistranslation of autism was affecting him to this day.

He sat at the courtroom at a loss for words when he realized that the police body camera was tampered with as well, sharing only a fraction of the confrontation to the room. In London, Kyron's behavior and skin color were translated to him being a threat and not useful for society. Fortunately for Kyron, his mom displayed perseverance by always advocating to the school board for Kyron to stay in school for as long as possible, and Kyron wanted to live up to his mom's example.

Kyron and I later discussed the seemingly night-and-day dynamics of having accommodation in school. Among Black autistics, I had the relatively rare experience of eventually receiving disability accommodation perfectly tailored for my needs when I later attended graduate school. I gasped when my disability and interview were approved and I was provided with a notetaker, extra time on tests, extra time to give presentations and vivas, and access to specialized tutoring and mentorship. I gasped at how my stress level decreased after my accommodation was implemented a few weeks into the school year. I swallowed any shyness or embarrassment I harbored about having a notetaker in our small class sizes, and was surprised at how little my 14 classmates seemed to notice or care. When Covid eventually disrupted our course, I was happy to see how all students—many of whom were likely experiencing an onset of symptoms like anxiety and depression for the first time—also received extra time to submit essays remotely. It reminded me of how freely accommodating those with undiagnosed disabilities can ultimately benefit the entire group.

Given such barriers of access to receive an autism diagnosis, and taking into account those like Kyron who receive a misdiagnosis of another condition, there are several possible ways universities can accommodate their students with minimal effort and financial cost. It is no secret that most student centers contain large rooms, often filled with lots of loud voices and other stimuli that may be overwhelming. In stark contrast, the quieter rooms in such centers are often reserved for studying, with minimal engagement allotted between students. The Neurodiversity Hub states that engaging with students, speaking explicitly, including tailored support services, and limiting the use of bright lights, loud noises, and open-floor planning are simple examples of enabling an inclusive work environment (Neurodiversity Hub, n.d.). Creating a diverse array of social and study environments for all personalities and neurotypes in student centers would enable a great first step in being more inclusive.

Additionally, while not accommodating those with unique needs (or waiting for a formal request to do so) can be detrimental, accommodating these needs can have a positive impact on all. An infamous example is the invention of SMS texts. Finnish inventors Matti Makkonen and colleagues originally invented SMS texting to be an alternative to voice conversations for deaf individuals and others who are hard of hearing. The use of SMS texting is now ubiquitous, as it proved to be efficient for both personal and professional use while also saving their intended company ample bandwidth. There are several other examples of accommodation to the minority that led to prosperity and convenience for the majority, ramps, elevators, and automatic doors being additional classic examples (Abrahams, n.d.).

It's evident that inclusive school settings lessen stress and decreases extreme mental health challenges. Accommodating those with diverse needs can also have a greater impact on the entire university community at large (Omeiza, 2021).

Kyron
London, England

After fighting to complete his GCSEs, Kyron now plans to later en-roll in a university. He was surprised at how relatively open schools can be for neurodivergent students like himself. But from his trauma with Ms. Trunchbull and beyond, he still struggles to share his work with others. Regardless, Kyron pushes to make sure his situation doesn't repeat in upcoming children in inner-city London and across England. As he has begun to heal from former attempts of being sidelined and excluded from school systems, he decided to speak out not to increase attention to himself, but to show-case attention to children who are too vulnerable to advocate for themselves.

Obtaining an education is already a form of resistance, and Kyron also started to advocate for others coming after him. He's currently a youth leader and community organizer for No More Exclusions, a Black youth-centered grassroots abolitionist coalition challenging high rates of disparities of school exclusions for marginalized com-munities. He leads group discussions, is a guest on various pod-casts, and engages others through his talent for poetry and story-telling. In a sign of true liberation, Kyron is also on the waiting list to receive his official autism assessment, although he self-identifies as autistic now. For him, and many others in London with his help, he is truly rewriting the status quo.

Shangwe
Moshi, Tanzania

"Usonji," a foreign doctor told Shangwe after conducting an as-sessment on Daniel in Tanzania. "It means autism," Shangwe ex-plained to my blank expression, "and he told me to read more on it." Shangwe did just that. In her new town in Moshi, she quickly connected with others who had autistic children, primarily to find out how she and Daniel could receive professional support. Upon further research, she realized that many families were taking full-day journeys for their weekly appointments in Moshi, often at obscure hours.

"Stigma is so high that most families hide their children indoors," Shangwe explained. Shortly after moving to Moshi, she realized that she didn't want to be one of the few to have the benefit of ease of healthcare access, so she created a group with other families to speak for the rights of autistic people to their community and the government. One year later, they founded a significant portion for Daniel and his new friends and named it the Li-TAFO Foundation. The Foundation also gives free transport for those who need to travel to the nation's capital for specialized healthcare. In 2022, they had a doctor from the capital come to conduct official autism assessments for those who could not travel and had not spoken to a doctor before.

As Shangwe told me of her recent success, I marveled at how we first became connected in the first place. She slid into my DMs (Direct Messages) to further discuss autism and Africa seeing that I lived on the continent for a small amount of time. Shangwe told me about the organization called Li-TAFO and how she was hoping to expand to be able to provide transportation to those in the community who needed support. Not fully understanding the transportation component of the organization, I gave her the small capital that I could and hoped it could add up when combined with other donations.

When I later asked her if she would like to be featured in this book, I was shocked at our subsequent interview when she explained to me how her organization was still in its nascency when she originally contacted me. I pondered at how simple it is to post on social media or sulk about hardships without a desire or plan to change. While it could rack up followers, it does very little for a situation and community that is affected by such hardships at large. Now a flourishing foundation that caters to several hundred people in a former resource-desert, Shangwe and Li-TAFO have truly laid the blueprint for rising above and taking action to support not only her family but also those around her. Shangwe and Daniel have received several national and international awards and press exposure for their work, and they're just getting started.

For Daniel, the effects of the Li-TAFO Foundation were immediate. He made new friends with others in his community, and the free transportation gave him access to see those friends as they pleased. After his mother's book launch with Tanzania's former prime minister, Daniel also receives priority visits with a therapist in order for him to heal from his former abuse. On his birthday, he is surrounded by loving community members, and those across the country and around the world have donated to the Li-TAFO Foundation on his behalf.

For Shangwe, starting the Li-TAFO Foundation with her son brought her peace. She soon discovered that many of the mothers were also divorcees due to their husbands abandoning their autistic children. Financing others' healthcare and school fees not only enabled the children to not be outcast from society, but showed community members that her happy family are human beings just like everyone else. Usonji, thanks to Shangwe and Daniel, was finally added to her region's vocabulary and no longer lost in translation. Quite literally, as the word is now added on official records such as the national census thanks to her and Daniel.

"I've raised awareness," Shangwe said, with Daniel grinning in the background. I was adjusting to her accent now, just as I did with Kyron's British accent in the remaining minutes just a couple of days before. "In the place I used to stay, they called me a witch. People no longer call me a witch anymore." She nodded at Daniel before concluding, "Yes, people no longer call me a witch anymore."

Ujima
Boston and Cambridge, Massachusetts, USA

"Hot Harvard blonde, right? Nah, mysterious brunette dude!" My intern friend and I joked while scrolling through Tinder over lunch. It was the early days of the Pokemon Go craze, and after the Harvard Medical School hospitals banned the game, the two of us decided to pass the time with dating apps instead. We pretended we were being ironic, but oftentimes we came into work at the brain imaging center excitedly swapping first date stories. Our giddiness made an appearance exclusively before working hours, during lunch, or when packing up to go home. During work? We felt trapped.

"Two children with nonverbal autism...can you imagine?" Our principal researcher reflected to us after my colleague and I underwent a mock brain scan with the children for an autism research study. She shook her head in pity as my colleague and I stared at her, reluctant to say anything that would set her off. The next part is honestly hazy in my memory but I believe she said something along the lines of "But good for us though...Kala's a pretty awkward girl, and talented at recruiting, perhaps you should put her in charge of getting the next participants, hopefully they'll be as efficiently on the spectrum as the previous ones." I, like others in my lab, felt isolated when being made to feel negatively about ourselves by our primary supervisor.

With Kyron and Shangwe, the public misconstruing autism nearly ruined their lives and those they loved. For me, I experienced how damaging stereotypes could be from some of those with the most power and influence over autistic individuals. On an internship at a nearby hospital the year before, I volunteered to have my brain scanned for one of the autism studies in a lab as a control sample. I happily volunteered, not considering that I could be autistic at the time. Now, or in the Pokemon Go era rather, it was my turn to be a full-time employee of this lab as a recent graduate, wide-eyed and eager to excel in a career in academia.

As the jabs rolled in, my intern friend and I quickly grew over-whelmed with the toxic environment led by our principal researcher. Weeks after starting the position, I resigned and volunteered at a suicidality lab at Harvard before taking on a full-time role at Duke Brain Imaging Analysis Center, where I would work with the most thoughtful and kind researcher and lab that one could ever ask for.

It was when I worked at Duke that I found out I was autistic. While I never formally told my new principal researcher, I knew she would have reacted kindly and would have even been happy for me to know more about myself. I was in a safe environment that valued mental health and the neurodivergent, and felt safe enough to challenge the way it all intersected with being a Black person. In the upcoming chapter, Danielle will overcome challenges in similar experiences, and begin to ask intersectional questions that I could only admire from afar during my time at Duke. The importance of being in a safe environment, without mistranslations of autism, is crucial for doing so.

As for my intern friend, she quit the lab a few months after me, withdrawing her honors thesis submission right before her final year as an undergrad. We would not see each other for another three years. To my surprise, it would be at a Masters program at Oxford. And to both of our surprise, we would then both be off dating apps for good. In a fancy library at an Oxford college, it would be where I learned that the creator of the original Pokemon was autistic.

"Of course he is," my [now former] intern friend said at lunch later that day. We both giggled as we shared our previous lab experience with the set of wide-eyed undergrads before us.

Chapter 7
Does My Black Life Matter?

Merced, California, USA • Philadelphia, Pennsylvania, USA

Dr. Maria Marten and Anani

Merced, California, USA

Anani first left her home country of Nigeria when she was 26 years old. She carried several duffel bags full of her favorite local foods and clothing fabric, in place of suitcases, hearing that her favorites would not be available nearly 8000 miles away. Anani was start-ing an interdisciplinary humanities course. She opted for several courses where she chose to study the intersection between Afri-can American and African cultures. For Anani, the knowledge gap she had regarding the history and the plight of African Americans since arriving as enslaved individuals in 1619 was wide. Although she had studied a little about African American literature and cul-ture during her university days in Nigeria, what she was exposed to in the courses she was offered at the University of California, Merced, made her feel that the historical African American knowl-edge that she had to learn was vaster than the miles that she had traveled across the Atlantic Ocean itself.

"I started having in-depth learnings about slavery, Jim Crow laws, lynchings…" Anani elaborated to me through voice messages. "All through history African Americans have had to work over twice as hard to 'prove themselves,' and even then struggled to get to the same level as white Americans. It was all very disturbing to learn." She was inspired by the likes of Martin Luther King, Martin Delany, Frederick Douglass, and others who sacrificed their lives and livelihoods for the betterment of their people. Still, Anani wants to encourage others who have a steep learning curve regarding Black history and also are learning about autistic individuals to put in the work just like she is regarding Black history at large.

Anani also struggled with the concept of what it means to be "Black" in the US. Back in Nigeria, she was used to others being described as "fair" or "dark." When she heard the description of Black being used in the US, she assumed it was a reference to those of a different ethnicity. "It took me a long time to fully understand that I'm also regarded as Black," Anani said, while chuckling. "I had to realize that that is the way [America] sees me, and that is how I'm classified." She also noted her interest in what it means to be an African American woman, or Black woman. Anani described to me that she felt that the impact of Black women's achievements and activism was particularly diminished or even erased from history, and she was interested in further discovering the extent of that erasure. Nevertheless, Anani described the categorization of white and Black to America's racist past as equating Black versus white to good versus evil. One, for example, is the rise of the Black Lives Matter Movement, its impact, its shortcomings, and its public perception.

Anani had a lot to learn about modern-day history as well. She was proud to understand the Black Lives Matter movement. "I see the Black Lives Matter movement as a very important movement, considering the ongoing hurdles of society," she told me. "It's the same 'Black and White' or racial bias mindset that leads people to see Black individuals as more likely to be criminals, and even being over three times more likely to be shot and killed by the police compared to white Americans," she said, referencing sources such as Harvard's School of Public Health 2020 article. "It's important that we fight for human dignity and our basic rights."

The history and modern-day dynamics of African Americans have understandably been a lot for Anani to take in. She finds herself studying longer than others to catch up on what her domestic peers consider "basic history" concerning slavery and Jim Crow laws. Dr. Maria Martin, an award-winning young professor, however, would soon give Anani and her fellow classmates new material and topics to ponder. Already flooded to the brim with notes and new head knowledge, Anani ordered new notebooks in anticipation of considering new insights in one of her favorite classes to date.

"In essence, I create an inclusive atmosphere where they are invited to recognize their need to unlearn some things, challenge some ideas they hold, and respectfully engage in learning about fellow human beings that have made important contributions to the world," Dr. Maria Martin explained to me on the phone. Dr. Maria Martin is a professor of history and critical race and ethnic studies at the University of California at Merced. For over five years, Dr. Martin has empowered her students to understand cultures outside of their own, not only for those such as Anani learning about African American culture, but those of many ethnicities learning about Anani's and other African cultures.

Dr. Martin's research and teaching stemmed from when she was once a graduate student like Anani. In those days, she took a class with a well-known professor of African history. They were dismayed by the end of the semester when their majority white class was still making ignorant statements about African people. The professor told Dr. Martin that they had failed their students. "I tried to be nice and say that they did all they could," Dr. Martin elaborated about her studentship days, "but when I became a professor, I realized my old professor did fail their students. In that class, there was no discussion of race and its relevance to African history."

"My classes, in essence, humanize Africa and therefore Black people in the eyes of my students and equip them to challenge ignorant notions among their peers and families that some students report. In this way, they learn how to become agents of change and allies by seeking to understand and respect people but not to otherize them." From her experience in that class and various classes before, Dr. Martin's current academic research interests are motivated by a desire to highlight the intellectualism, activism, and importance of African and African-descended people.

Dr. Martin's class that Anani enrolled in was titled "Transnational Black Feminism". In that class, Dr. Martin discussed more about the issues of race and struggles of liberation that are unavoidable in the Black feminist canon. Regarding the Black Lives Matter Movement, Dr. Martin described to me that while this movement is a part of the long history of freedom movements and actions by Black people, BLM was founded by Patrisse Cullors, Ayo Tometi, and Alicia Garza in the aftermath of George Zimmerman's (the man who murdered Black teen Trayvon Martin in 2012) acquittal. "In fact," Dr. Marin added, "The Black women who founded BLM are in a long line of Black women activists from Baeffu—who led a slave rebellion in the Danish West Indies in 1733—to Harriet Tubman, Mary McLeod Bethune, Mamie Till, Rosa Parks and the southern women who started the Civil Rights Movement, the Black women who ran the programs and newspaper of the Black Panther Party, and so on."

Dr. Martin informed me of her thoughts on the Black Lives Matter Movement's progress, and ways it could improve.

"I think that BLM has made its presence felt and has caused good changes across policing, education, and entertainment. For example, in policing there has been legislative change such as Breonna's Law which bans no-knock warrants, the repeal of 50-A which made police behavior records unavailable to the public, and policies restricting the use of the chokehold among other things. However, the movement struggles with the erasure and silencing of Black women in BLM. Black women experience the same maltreatment as men in terms of shootings, police stops, and racial profiling. I have had harrowing experiences with the police myself!! On two separate occasions I thought I was going to die at their hands. Black women also suffer gendered violence from police such as when former officer Daniel Holtzclaw preyed on Black women and raped them. These stories of Black women are not always recognized and this is precisely why the African American Policy Forum and the Center for Intersectionality and Social Policy Studies started the #SayHerName campaign in 2014. It addressed the erasure of women in BLM. The two organizations wanted to bring attention to the fact that Black women have been targets of, have suffered from, and died because of racism as well."

In addition, Dr. Martin discussed her parallels of "otherism" in various groups in intersectionalities. Dr. Martin described how the

Black women activists throughout African American history have been fighting against what she calls the organizing principles of US society. In her words, organizing principles are those deeply embedded but silent ideas that shape the way that people operate and think in society.

"In the US there are two prevailing principles that organize society: (1) white supremacist capitalism and (2) biological determinism. The first is a system that has historically and contemporarily privileged white males in the society as the most powerful and important beings. The second has tied certain characteristics and traits to biological differences. This leads to ideas that can create inequality and hierarchies such as those that subject women to men—because they are biologically different than men—or ideas that subject Black people to white people (because one group is seen as more intellectual, civilized, creative, and superior than the other). BLM is a part of a long line of activists that have been fighting the negative effects of these organizing principles," she added.

Anani has been inspired by Dr. Martin's commitment to what she does and how she integrates creativity into her classes. "She models activism, and emulates how Black feminists, like those before her, can make a difference." Many of Dr. Martin's students have benefited from her teachings and furthered their understanding of anti-Blackness in the US in particular. Anani, for example, has taken a keen interest in further understanding Dr. Martin's second organizing principle, biological determinism.

Anani began reading about the disability rights movements, and how they often ran in parallel to Black rights movements in the US and even around the world. Anani referred to my second novel *The Worst Saturday Ever* when describing how non-disabled individuals, neurotypicals, and others often regard themselves as superior to those who don't consider themselves so, such as autistic individuals.

"This is a really important point [you made]," Anani said when referencing the part of my novel that describes an autistic Black man telling an autistic Black teenage boy how the world wants them to assimilate and act exactly like the majority to not be perceived as a threat. Anani now understood that perceived threat was the case for African Americans and Black people like herself, but what about the impact of those such as Black individuals with intersectional identities such as being autistic and Black? Disabled and Black? To find out, Anani utilizes Dr. Martin's sage instructions on promoting inclusivity to further and understanding tailored to the historical background as well as modern trials and progress of what it means to not only be a Black woman, but an autistic one as well in today's times. Fortunately, Dr. Martin provided me with the cheat sheet ahead of time by further informing me on the topic.

"Activists, feminists, and scholars have been discussing the links between ableism (privileging able bodied people in society), race, and rights for the disabled for some time, though much work needs to be done before their message is concretized in the actions of the society.... This is made apparent when considering findings of the Center for American Progress which state that at least 50 percent of people killed by police in the USA are disabled. However, when that person is Black and disabled, they face more danger. According to the World Disability Institute, 50 percent of Black disabled people are arrested by the time that they are 28 years old and many of the high profile murders of Black people by police were highly influenced by the disability of the deceased. Black disabled people face more of a threat in the USA because the racial hierarchy in the US ties ideas of criminality to Blackness. This means that any misunderstood behaviors done by Black disabled people are viewed as criminal before any consideration is given to the ways that their disability affects them. In addition, since Black people experience high rates of poverty and have long survived in resource deficient areas in the USA, those with disabilities have even less of a chance to have a good quality of life in these areas because their needs are not likely to be addressed. According to the World Disability Institute, even in times of disaster the needs of disabled Black people are not considered in preparation, rescue, and recovery.

Though this presents a bleak picture for Black disabled people in the USA, there have been people fighting for disabled rights as a part of Black liberation. The historical relationship between Black liberation and disabled rights is not often at the forefront of conversations about Black history but they are linked. For example, Bradley Lomax, who was a Black Panther and founder of the East Oakland Center for Independent Living (also supported by the Panthers), was wheelchair bound due to multiple sclerosis. According to Independence Now, an advocate for disabled rights, the Panthers supported section 504 of the Rehabilitation Act which gave protections to disabled people by granting access to benefits and services funded by federal accounts. It also forbade discrimination by employers. This was important for the later Americans with Disabilities Act (ADA). The act passed but the Federal government still had to be forced to implement it, so Lomax and 119 others staged a sit in at the US Department of Health, Education and Welfare building in San Francisco. They were given food by the Panthers which helped them to sustain their movement. It was successful, lasted 25 days, and was the longest sit-in at a federal building to date according to Independence Now.

It would bring more attention to the interconnections of Black history and disabled history in the USA if the disabilities of Black icons were revealed. For example, Harriet Tubman suffered with seizures throughout her life and activism after being hit in the head with a piece of iron thrown by a slave catcher as a little child. According to the US Department of Labor, Civil Rights leader Fannie Lou Hamer, who was a fierce advocate for Black voting rights and co-founder of the Mississippi Freedom Democratic Party, had polio as a child and suffered a beating at the hands of police for her activism which left her with a limp, kidney damage, and sight loss. According to the National Endowment for the Humanities, she was also sterilized without her consent in what is referred to as a Mississippi appendectomy and she lost a daughter because no hospital in Mississippi would treat a child of Fannie Lou Hamer. Barbara Jordan, the first Black woman to be elected to the US House of Representatives, had multiple sclerosis and Johnnie Lacy who made strides for the Independent Living Movement was paralyzed from polio at 19 according to the US Department of Labor. There are many more Black and disabled icons and activists that show the indelible connection between race or Blackness and rights for the disabled."

In academia several years behind Dr. Martin, Anani is now used to implementing her share of readings and research to catch up to her peers. She's thankful for mentors like Dr. Martin to lay the template of how to do so. Anani plans to gather qualitative evidence, or personal stories. To do this, she's broadened her network to platform voices like Danielle's.

Danielle
Philadelphia, Pennsylvania, USA

In Philadelphia, PA, USA, Danielle Pierre struggles to find a community where she feels fully included. Danielle self-diagnosed as autistic.

Like Anani, Danielle was raised in a different culture, by her parents who were immigrants from Trinidad and Grenada. Unlike Anani, however, Danielle grew up in the USA, fully immersed in its dynamics. Still, Danielle's autistic traits began to bother her parents as well as many others from early on in her life.

"I was a crybaby," Danielle said, chuckling briefly before frowning. "But it was always seen as 'you don't have control of your emotions'. Crying or meltdowns was always seen as a bad thing. They perceived the way I showed emotions as weak." Like many Black parents, Danielle later realized that her parents wanted her to be in the best position to succeed in life and in their new life in the USA. Being Black was already a hindrance, so being Black and acting differently than others would already place Danielle behind, which frightened her parents.

"They were always like 'How are you going to make it in the world if you're so sensitive?' And so I kind of have that critical voice in the back of my head still to this day," she added.

Danielle identifies as queer, and has struggled with both platonic and romantic relationships. She has selective mutism on occasion, where she doesn't speak, especially in times of stress. When she tried to become close with others, she found herself being stigmatized before saying a single word.

"At University for example—at a PWI [Primarily White Institution]—my classmates would see me as just a Black girl who's not speaking. I think a lot of people can think I just have an attitude and don't care…. Whereas I'm like, literally shaking in my boots cause I'm so scared and nervous. I don't know how to communicate and I'm overwhelmed," Danielle said. She later left school before graduation. She felt that her struggling to understand herself and how people interacted with her contributed to her not performing well academically.

Danielle was also confused on why she struggled to fit in with her Black peers.

"In the Black community, there is a tendency to view weakness or social feebleness as a crime," Danielle said in a separate conversation. "'How are we going to make it in this world?' That is the wrong question. The question is why do we live in a world that views these characteristics as weakness? How can we live in a world that is radically accommodating and accepting of neurodiversity?" Danielle spoke further to me about how there was a divide in how the few Black people in her living area at university understood her. Similarly to Anani, she wondered if it was because she grew up in a different background than her peers. Danielle grew up primarily around recent Black and Brown immigrants, and her Black peers at University grew up in predominantly white suburbia and had issues of classism, sizeism, colorism, etc. However, she later came to realize that she was ostracized mainly because of her behaviors, which she would later come to understand are an aspect of her autistic traits. Having selective mutism and engaging in elopement, for example, didn't help matters. When she did speak, speaking in unconventional prosody would be enough to drive those remaining away.

It wasn't until Danielle was reading about African spirituality that she fully came to terms with being autistic. To paraphrase, she had the following to say. "I discovered the Yoruba religion of *ifa*, and spiritual beings related to *egbe* and *akibu*. It was fascinating learning about how *ifa* and spiritual beings related to *egbe* seemed to relate almost directly to both children and adults with autism and ADHD in particular. Apparently, children born of *egbe* were seen as those that made a covenant with the spiritual realm to stay on earth. When those on earth fail to realize their covenant, they can experience challenges and symptoms that I believe to be similar to those of autistic people."

The terminology of African spirituality is no doubt provocative and controversial for some autistics that have heard about it, but Danielle seemed to find it interesting. She said "Now [after learning more about spirituality] I'm realizing that my discomfort is something that needs to be investigated. And it's a reflection of how the outside world treats me for who I am. So it's made me a little bit stronger in that aspect. I now feel like I don't have to criticize myself for not connecting with people. And I also kind of view autism a little more as a gift. It's a painful gift, but that's a form of discernment as well."

Danielle and I informally discussed my perspective during the Black Lives Matter Movement that formed when I was in undergrad in the USA, and received worldwide attention by the time I was in graduate school in the UK. In the USA, I shared similar sentiments as Danielle. She and I chuckled in commiseration as I told her about how I often participated in protests in college, but whenever I portrayed autistic traits, like repeatedly misunderstanding directions, I was both scoffed at and laughed at. My most stark memory of the phenomenon occurred when, days after a large protest that I happily participated in, and several months after my suicide attempt, my mother encouraged me to form a connection with the "nonner" Black students that I engaged in activism with. Scared and afraid to not fit in, I protested, but my loving mother suggested I take my favorite hobby with me—reading—to encourage conversation.

Still scared, I did just that. I went to the new diversity affairs center with a novel, and sat in one of the couches among other Black and Brown students. I received many side-eyes, but also a few nods, probably in recognition of my appearance at protests. In my nervousness, I failed to say anything to the brief eye contact that the nodding heads gave me. On the verge of a panic attack, I hurried out of the center. All I had to show for that experience was chuckled rumors about me and a novel read two sentences further.

Danielle, on the other hand, is now in the process of returning to finish university. As she is healing from misunderstanding and blaming herself, she has taken plenty of time to reflect on society and how it can be better for those like her. Of course, Danielle loves being Black, and loves the diversity in the Black community. She supports the sentiments behind the Black Lives Matter Movement:

"Black lives *do* matter."

However, in recent years, Danielle has witnessed that the individuals that have ostracized her and continue to do so are adamant about the movement as well. She worries that that is the dominant sentiment, one where she's wondering:

"*Which* Black lives matter?"

Danielle and I discussed the importance of our Black community embracing intersectionalities like being both Black and autistic. She spoke about how she did not feel included as an autistic person in the Black Lives Matter movement. We discussed how neurotypical society requires social ease and extroversion, and how it's discomforting for many neurotypical people to interact with someone who isn't complying to the social communication standards, which is common for many disabled and/or autistic people. Adding skin color and sexual orientation specifically makes this disconnect even more stark. She made a thoughtful remark for all individuals to embrace.

"We all need to learn to love the outcasts. Approach them with grace, dignity, and an outstretched hand, not just as an empty gesture of niceness, but as a recognition of their humanity."

"Disability and desirability are interconnected," she continues, "those who are undesirable or ugly, we regard them as less than human. Graces are not spared and they are easily disposable. No community is immune to this. But it is possible to divorce desirability from human worth. Autistic people do it all the time. To many autistics, it is the content and depth of connection that makes life worth living. Everything else is superfluous. If the Black community as a whole were to switch to that autistic mode of thinking, we would be a lot further as a people.

[To do this, we need to] return to who we were. Learn more about who we come from. Learn more about who we revered, how we lived. How free we were. And bring some of the past to the present with us."

Dr. Maria Martin and Anani
Merced, California, USA

At the time of this writing, Anani was unpacking her bags in Cambridge, MA. She once again brought her duffle bags as she began a summer research fellowship at Harvard. There was a lot of history to catch up on regarding African Americans in the North East, such as the great migration that Dr. T described early in the book, as only one of several examples. For the first time, Anani was excited to read and learn more about what it means to be a Black neuro-divergent woman in particular and their hidden stories throughout history. Certainly, there were more narratives like Danielle's that were missing. It is clear to see that there is work to be done in our Black community to make sure that all Black lives matter. To do so, it's time that we begin to listen to those that feel that their lives do not.

Anani has been proud of herself as she's opened her mind to the topic of Black Lives Matter, and encourages others new to the subject to do the same. As her historical knowledge base catches up to Danielle's and Dr. Martin's, she realizes that there are still more nuances to understand. For example, she found that Harvard had a larger supply of Nigerian food ingredients compared to Merced, as well as her cultural fabrics. Anani knew, of course, that Nigerian immigration history and culture, much like Danielle's Trinidadian background, and its specific dynamics towards disabled individuals, was a story for another day. Onward, to a journey of analyzing the Black Lives Matter Movement and its intersectionality with gender and disability.

Ujima
Durham, North Carolina, USA

At Duke's campus, near my new lab, I took a deep breath as I finally entered the location of their Graduate Christian Fellowship. I had been working at Duke for at least four months before I gathered the courage to do so, as I realized I needed more people in my life, like my college friend Allyson, who shared my values.

The leader of the fellowship, a cell biology Ph.D. student recently turned professor, welcomed me with open arms. Sure, I wasn't technically a grad student yet, but the fact that I wanted to be soon, and related with that demographic, allowed me to fit in with their target audience. I'm sure Danielle would have loved attending some of the lectures and book discussions about racism within a religious community. The fellowship leader was always intentional about centering Black voices and allowing tough conversational topics like racism to come into an otherwise homogeneous space. Like Danielle, however, I was looking forward to having my first group of Black friends as an adult, and actively sought out new friends.

There weren't a large number of Black graduate students at Duke, and those that attended the Christian fellowship were a small minority. While the fellowship leader was a great ally, I relished the opportunity to connect with more Black individuals outside of the Duke community. I later gathered the courage to join a few MeetUp groups meant for Black professionals. One of them became one of the most traumatizing experiences of my life.

I reduced my rate of attending the Christian fellowship bi-monthly as I became hyper involved with the new group. Excited about having Black friends, I fixated on learning everything about them, and volunteered to help organize events and charitable outreaches. However, my eyes were opened as wide as Anani and Danielle's when I had what was in hindsight a serious meltdown, and was quickly ostracized from that group and everyone in it. My subsequent suicide attempt was scoffed at as a cry for attention by those who advocated for the liberation of Black lives. And some, including those practicing or studying medicine and psychology, who I felt should have had the training and the emotional skills to be more empathetic, said they decided to formally block me from all online and offline activities. They felt that I could possibly hurt them one day after witnessing my meltdown. The niece that Dr. T mentioned in Chapter 4? Yeah, that was unfortunately me.

For a while, I was resentful of them and of my former Boston Principal Researcher (my supervisor who led me to resign after only after a few months because of the toxic working environment): those that had potential power and privilege over the Black and/or autistic community. I was bitter about them repeating the cycle of emotional abuse that I am sure they themselves endured. My emotional abusers had experienced life as a woman graduate student in science a few decades ago, or had grown up in the modern-day USA as Black people with their own experiences of oppression and microaggressions. Like I have done myself several times before, I know that it is easier to repeat the past when a new type of person comes into the present. I am grateful for the growth I've made in allowing myself to grow outside of my own box, and I am thankful for the increasing discernment to allow empathy for other groups who I did not know previously. That in itself makes me feel hopeful that, like me, some of those in that group would have the time and grace to learn and grow as well over the weeks, years, or decades. With others beginning to grow at a speed varying from a cheetah to a snail, the future of intersectional tolerance and acceptance has nowhere to go but up.

After I humbly crawled back to the fellowship, and explained to the leaders what had happened during my disappearance, the fellowship leader gasped in horror at my retelling of the events of the highly charged few months. When I was diagnosed with autism a few months later, the fellowship leader, the few Black students in the fellowship, and a new Bible study I joined all stood by me on a walk for autism awareness and acceptance. It was the unexpected negative experience from a Black advocacy group, and the equally unexpected allyship from my Christian groups, that made me decide that the world was in more need of intersectional advocacy from diverse individuals. My lifelong friendship with the fellowship leader and others inspired me to start my own mental health advocacy initiatives. One day, they will hopefully be on the same level and stage as the organizations founded by those in the following chapter.

Chapter 8
An Impi in Advocacy

Akha
Pretoria, South Africa

Dear Readers,

Today I'm going to talk about falling in love. Now before you get all excited let me clarify. I am not talking about romantic love. The type of love I am talking about is the love you feel when someone really gets you.

I remember how I used to feel when everyone thought I was low functioning. I was so sad and lost. I thought that no one would ever see me and that I would be trapped forever. But my wonderful mother never gave up on me.

I was taken to see Tracy Gunn who is a speech therapist. She is trained to work with nonspeaking autistics. She sees me. She understands my body and respects my brain. She fights to make sure I get a good education and she finds friends for me. I love her so much.

My wish is that every nonspeaking autistic can find a Tracy. Someone who fights for them and gives them a voice.

Until next time
Akha

Love, September 6th 2019 (Akha Kumalo, n.d.)

"I am a Zulu, and we are proud and fierce people," Akha said. He's 12 years old and living in Pretoria, South Africa. As South Africa is home to nine major ethnic groups and ten official languages, Zulu is counted as one of the largest tribes and languages in the country (South Africa, n.d.).

Akha loves learning about the history of the Zulu people and African history in general. As a nonspeaker, he informed me of his favorite hobbies and activities by using a letterboard through the International Association of Spelling to Communicate (I-ASC, n.d.).

"I am proud of our legacy," Akha said, referring to his Zulu heritage. With further research, I learned that Shaka was one of the greatest Zulu chiefs in the 19th century. He conquered multiple territories that eventually encompassed the Zulu empire. Starting as the leader of one of the smallest clans in size at the beginning of his reign, Shaka designed an infamous military tactic to separate the soldiers by age groups, represented by headdresses and shield designs among others. Together, these soldiers formed an impi, where they covered over 50 miles a day to exterminate nearby clans. The strongest of the soldiers symbolized the "chest", and would be the first to close in on the enemy. The more agile would surround the foe and attack the enemy from behind. The strengths and weaknesses of each part of the impi collaborated to defeat neighboring clans throughout Shaka's reign, leading to a series of events that made the Zulu one of the most populous tribes in South Africa today (Morris, 2019).

Shaka's impi tactic enforced an equitable and resourceful utilization of the soldiers' inherent strengths. Rather than leaving smaller and younger soldiers vulnerable to capture and attacks, the impi tactic utilized their agility to strengthen the group as a whole.

In the 21st century, however, reverse tactics have been in play that leave differing civilians excluded, and exposed to various attacks from modern-day society, such as lack of access to education, resources, and community.

As an extroverted nonspeaking, autistic pre-teen, Akha feels the desire to mingle and bring joy to those around him. However, most underestimate his abilities. Since utilizing the letterboard to communicate, Akha says that being able to assertively communicate to others more effectively has made him able to advocate for a better education and social life. "It has opened up my whole world," Akha said regarding the letterboard. He has been able to utilize his gift for writing and the love of people and his culture to teach others about those with differing needs. With people like Akha, there's hope that modern-day societies can form a peaceful version of the cohesive impi.

Gerald
Raleigh, North Carolina, USA

"If I rob a bank, can I tell the police I did so because I'm autistic? Of course not!" Gerald said, leaning forward with his shoulders raised. Gerald was talking about a time when a fellow autistic individual was bothering him. They are both a part of an advocacy/hang-out group in Raleigh, North Carolina, partially spear-headed by Gerald himself. For Gerald, he feels that he has come a long way with having compassion for and getting to know himself. With people of differing abilities, he has learned he, like everyone, has more learning to do.

Gerald received an autism diagnosis at three years old. He went to several different schools across the South Eastern United States as his parents traveled. Now 36, Gerald recalled how he struggled to fit in and find a community at any of those schools, mainly because he felt that his specific needs didn't fit in with either side of the spectrum. His parents, for example, didn't consider autism to be a disability, so neither did he. As a student with special needs, he was enrolled in primarily special education classes, and had a hard time finding his place.

"You have those who fit in with the special needs kids and those with the neurotypical kids. I knew I was in the middle and that my case was unique," Gerald recalled. He swayed back and forth on the screen when he spoke to me, his swaying accelerating and voice raising as he discussed topics in which he was more interested.

As he approached middle and high school, he learned that he could mask or conceal his autistic traits, and so he did. He went to a charter middle school in North Carolina, followed by a boarding school in Mississippi for high school. He was grateful that the schools were diverse and had a wide array of people he could mirror and belong with. During those days, Gerald never revealed his autism diagnosis to his peers or community members, as he was nervous about the ramifications of being left out and alone. His passion for drawing was largely kept undisclosed so as to not bring his hyperfocused interests to attention. He also stopped receiving reasonable accommodation during his teen years and he didn't feel he needed it. As the schools were more funded, he enjoyed the smaller class sizes that made it more tolerable to learn in the standard environment. He was also sure to stick with smaller class sizes when he went to college.

Alex
Tennessee, USA

The American South includes most of where Gerald lived and schooled, including North Carolina. The southern part of the country is filled with much beauty and history and generally holds relatively conservative views. In Tennessee, for example, I spoke with an individual with the alias Alex about how they were forced to enroll in a social skills debutante class to keep up with the "southern belle" aesthetic.

"People here don't say they're autistic, they say 'they're not autistic, they're just special, a late bloomer' even if autism is a label that the person likes," Alex said. Because of this, Alex was told to not speak about their condition. They recalled how their family was upset that the social skills debutante class didn't "cure their autism" as their family had hoped. "They always wanted me to play with the other girls. And I just enjoyed playing by myself," Alex said.

As a mixed raced nonbinary individual who was raised by white parents, Alex had a hard time fitting in with their classmates and surroundings. Even while attempting to utilize the skills from the social skills debutante class, they struggled to fit in with their peers. Alex's family signed them up for a cheerleading team, of which they noticed a serious racial divide. Trying to fit in with the Black cheerleaders, Alex was often picked on and called out for not being "cultured".

"There were all sorts of jokes about my lack of culture," Alex said. "When I tried to adapt by making the same jokes back, it didn't work. I never got the whole mimicking thing down. I was never able to grasp that it took a certain amount of closeness with people who have these jokes."

With the pushback Alex observed about being autistic, their experience with the southern common social skills debutante class had made them feel as if the traits, mannerisms, and comfort they had were inherently wrong. Instead of reaching out to their local community, Alex relies on advocacy initiatives online. Alex follows autism groups and blogs by people of all abilities, but is drawn to those that have other marginalized identities.

Just like there is a vast range of diversity in people, thought, and culture across the American South, there is also diversity across the autism spectrum. A southern belle in their own right, Alex hopes that they would soon see further advocates represent and reflect the diverse human race.

Gerald
Raleigh, North Carolina, USA

In North Carolina, Gerald decided it was time to take a stand. After college, Gerald began to slowly unveil his mask. He sought to learn more about autism and what it means to different people who are diagnosed, and the professionals who care for them. Once again, he found himself in the middle of most of the debates. Unlike some advocates, he didn't see autism as a superpower or an entity that should be fully labeled as a strength. He also agreed with his family in that he didn't see it as a weakness, or a disability in itself. He discussed with me the flawed medical model of autism, which essentially sees the condition as a list of impairments or deficits. Firmly in the middle, Gerald wished more professionals expressed viewpoints like his.

"There's something different with my brain," he said, regarding his definition of autism. "It doesn't mean that I have a bad brain though. There's nothing to fix," he said, his swaying accelerating. Gerald's swaying continued to accelerate as he discussed the autism advocacy group he leads. He initially joined the advocacy group after he was experiencing burnout in his new job in Raleigh. "I was doing more than what my brain would allow me to do," he said, his eyes lowered and his swaying stiffened. He enjoyed networking and connecting with other autistic people who shared his experience. Newly unashamed to unveil his mask, he became one of the leaders a few months after he joined the organization when one of the previous leaders stepped down.

Gerald loves connecting with people face-to-face. Events he led with the autism group included adult arcade outings, and visits to several restaurants, movie theaters, and parks. His favorite were the art museums where he was able to be his full self by outwardly appreciating the beauty of drawings specifically. For the most part, most of the autistic individuals had temperaments and mannerisms similar to him. The vast majority were male, and he mostly found himself being the only Black individual. When a second Black man joined, he was at first joyous of the likelihood of having more in common with his experience, but Gerald had to quickly learn to adapt to the notion that autism is indeed a spectrum of conditions.

Gerald and the new member got along well at first, the new member was very friendly and would be in communication with Gerald regularly. However, Gerald quickly began to feel irritated when the individual started to message and call him several times a day on various platforms. When Gerald tried to enforce boundaries, he found that he was being accused of disliking him or not being friendly himself.

A meticulous follower of rules, Gerald wanted to be strict about the aim of the advocacy group. To him, the aim of the group and the accompanying Facebook group was to share events going on in the autism advocacy space at large, and discuss ideas about autism advocacy specifically. He heavily enforced this rule, starting by leaving a comment on the Facebook post of the offender as an initial warning, a private message as a second warning, and resulting in dropping the offender from the group if the matter continued. Gerald enforced these guidelines without discrimination, often priding himself on how his rigidness is seen as a strength in this instance.

The new Black autistic member broke all rules with haste, and Gerald swiftly enforced his guidelines while disregarding the budding friendship both he and the new member thought they had. Eventually, Gerald removed him from the advocacy and Facebook group. It only took a couple of days for the white members to protest against the group that the new individual was being discriminated against by his race and support needs. Understandably, Gerald was confused about this accusation as a Black male who required accommodation for part of his childhood. Feeling that his views were correct, Gerald doubled down.

"I responded to the protests that maybe the group isn't accessible to [the new individual]," Gerald said, his swaying starting to slowly pick up. The protests increased with that response, and accusations that Gerald was being ableist were piling up even on private posts on accounts outside of the group. Confused, Gerald resumed what he had started months ago and researched more about autism and how it is portrayed in different people. He learned that it was up to him and the other leaders of the group to become more accessible and accommodating to recruit, support, and uplift other autistic individuals that didn't fit the mold as he did.

"Yeah, some things I said might have come off strong or blunt to other people back then, but I didn't mean to come off that way," he reflected. His swaying increased as he shared with me how autistic individuals with varying support needs all have different pros and cons. While Gerald has the privilege of masking at this point of his life, he's noticed that he's often disregarded and sometimes not believed he is autistic by the public and even professionals.

"People don't think I'm autistic because I don't behave like their nonspeaking son," he said, "which is unfair. But it's also unfair to think that people that have higher support needs are not capable of learning and growing too." Gerald took it upon himself to make amends with his recently banished new member. While he didn't feel one could get away with breaking the rules just because of their abilities, he knew he needed to take ownership to communicate his boundaries in an accessible manner. He had a comprehensive discussion about the group rules, and the new member agreed to hold most social or casual conversations offline of the group going forward.

"Maybe I don't understand how [the new member] and others experience the world or how they see things," he said, "but I know you can't classify people as capable or incapable by what you see." He discussed how, like the rest of the population, we all have something we need more support with or need to work on about ourselves. For Gerald, it was about adapting to change. During the lockdown periods of 2020–2021, Zoom became popular for meet-ups, even though Gerald preferred to meet in person. He learned to see the benefits of increased online usage, such as how he noticed more autistic voices, including women, nonbinary people, and people of color were being heard. When the lockdown period ended, Gerald enforced a hybrid model to keep including social events. For in person, he enforced social distancing measures that have also been good for many of his group members.

The Raleigh-Durham autism advocacy group ultimately became stronger when a more diverse array of autistic individuals was made comfortable to be involved. Now, Gerald openly discusses his love for drawing in person and virtually hears feedback and opinions from those he otherwise wouldn't have met. Thanks to the new member, protestors, and Gerald for persevering to do the hard work of advocating and implementing inclusivity for all, the group enjoys the strength in diversity they have. Gerald beamed and swayed at the mention that he was indeed running a modern-day impi.

Akha
Pretoria, South Africa

A few thousand miles away, Akha continued to discuss with me his family life and favorite activities. His favorite people in the world are his family members, and his best friend Tyler. "My sister is the other of my soul," Akha said, "And Tyler is awesome." Watching videos and reading with his mom, sister, and friend truly make his world fun and whole.

While the 12-year-old prepares to become a historian to study African cultures like his Zulu tribe, he's spent most of his young life observing the harsh reception of him as a nonspeaking autistic boy with high support needs.

"I am a very social person," Akha said, "but it's really hard to make friends when you have a silly body like mine. I want to connect so badly but people don't understand me so they shy away. It is so hurtful." As his speech therapist interpreted the letterboard, Akha shouted many terms such as "enough" and "no" abruptly, possibly referring to his "silly body" as his impaired motor and speech mannerisms. Akha continued to pace, stim, and say and shout words throughout the interview while relying on the letterboard and his speech therapist to interpret what was truly on his mind.

Akha started blogging when he was nine years old. He told me about how passionate he is about being an activist for nonspeakers, and how he hopes to reach other nonspeakers and families with nonspeakers so they can find their voices and be better understood. Akha did not have a method to communicate before the letterboard. "Spelling to communicate has opened up my whole world," Akha said, he stimmed and shouted a bit while the speech therapist interpreted what he had typed on the letterboard.

Akha blogs about what it is like to live as a nonspeaking individual, an individual who is often spoken over by neurotypical parents and speaking autistic people alike. He advocates for nonspeakers' right to be treated like humans and to belong to their community. Akha is thankful he can utilize his gift of writing to help bring nonspeakers onboard to the impi of autism advocacy, while simultaneously putting himself as an asset to the impi of overall modern society. Just like Gerald swaying increased when he talked about his advocacy, Akha's stimming increased in between typing on his letterboard when he talked about his blog.

"I want the world to know that I am just like you. I may seem different, but inside I am just the same," Akha said when I asked him what he wanted others to know about him most. "I think. I feel. I dream. I hope. I laugh. Take the time to get to know me. Don't judge me by my outside. There is," he grunted and stimmed a bit before continuing "There is so much more to me."

Akha's movement has received attention nationwide. He has given multiple presentations, including one to over 50 teachers and educators in South Africa. With his job as a historian a few years away, the pre-teen enjoys advocating for himself and others to make both the autism and community at large a better place. "There is so much more work still to be done," he concluded, "but I think I've [so far] changed some hearts."

Akha, Gerald, and Alex represent just a fraction of the diversity of the Black autism population. Utilizing one's talent as a nonspeaker like Akha, and learning to understand and value their true self like Alex are examples to follow for making both themselves and their communities better. Being adaptive, communicative, and inclusive like Gerald, is often tough for most, but it's nonetheless essential for making room for those who are unable to mask and are often overlooked. As the three individuals know, the Black community is only stronger together. *When the Black, autistic community comes together, that truly will be a dynamic and peaceful impi.*

Dear Readers,

Today I want to talk about respecting autistic people. People think that because some autistics can't speak, they are low functioning but this is not true. The only reason they are not speaking is because they have motor planning difficulties. This is interfering with their ability to speak. Let me assure you that they would talk if they could.

The way you treat them is so important. Imagine that you were smart but trapped in your body. Imagine if people spoke to you as if you were a baby. How would that make you feel? That is how the autistic person feels all the time.

Let them know that you see them in there. The thought that they are not seen is frightening. So scary that you might be missed. So scary that you might be trapped in your body forever and no one will ever see you.

Then, when you speak to them, let them know that you know that they are smart. Be respectful of their brains and talk to them like you would talk to anyone of their age. Talk to them about interesting things. Never talk to them like a baby.

Until next time,
Akha

Akha, Respecting Autistics, July 19th 2019 (Akha Kumalo, n.d.)

Ujima
Ibadan, Nigeria

"It won't fit," I shrugged when trying on a pair of jeans. I was in Nigeria and West Africa for the first time as a US Fulbright Scholar researching suicidality in Christian and ethnic contexts. I loved my experience working with a brilliant professor at University of Ibadan and at the World Health Collaboration Center. However, my main aim was to get to know those in my demographic in this new environment. I lived on the medical campus, and a few of my new friends took me to a market to try on a new outfit for a proper Nigerian birthday celebration.

The jeans, in fact, did fit. After rejoicing in finding the perfect pair that were at least four sizes too large, my friends laughed at the sight and proceeded to help me negotiate the original pair for a few hundred naira.

"I don't understand, don't Americans like jeans too?" my psychiatry student friend asked later. My dental student friend, replying on my behalf, said something like "Americans don't like a lot of things, like eye contact." For the sake of my own benefit of fitting in, I often let it go when my friends and neighbors assumed that my autistic traits were simply American traits.

In Nigeria, I experienced a similar phenomenon as Akha in the previous chapter—I was seen as an outsider among those who did share my skin color. While I relished the med student friends I made when living at the hospital, I had encountered several scenarios where I was also seen as American first before anything else. One was in the way I wore my hair. While some like my dental student friend were in the process of growing out their permed hair, full afros were a rare sight in Ibadan at the time, signaling that you may be a villager that specifically practices witchcraft (not my words), or a foreigner who primarily resides in and around the major nearby city of Lagos. In language, I realized that high-context countries like Nigeria, in which communication is done by shared meanings and cues rather than explicit words, were a sure fire situation to enable misunderstandings among foreigners. I once wrote in my blog shortly after such an encounter, titled "Beauty and The Beans":

> My cleaner and I have never been the best communicators with each other. She told me her name once, but I have no idea how to pronounce it or spell it, so I'll refrain from trying on this platform. She comes into my room to clean nearly every day, and the days when I'm in my room we manage to greet each other quickly, as we've learned that neither of us can understand each other when we attempt to go into a more complex sentence such as "How was your day?"

> Nonetheless, she's always so surprised and enthralled when I greet her with a Yoruba greeting, and I'm pleasantly surprised when I hear her say something in American vernacular such as "What's up?"

> One day, I walked past the cleaner when I was walking to work. She looked absolutely stunning in a traditional dress.

> I smiled at her and told her that she looked beautiful.

> "Heh?"she responded, not understanding what I meant.

> "YOU LOOK BEAUTIFUL!" I shouted in the classic ignorant American manner to become louder when people can't understand our English.

"HEH?!"

"Ewa!" I finally said, translating to "beautiful" in Yoruba.

My cleaner shrugged, pointed to the cafeteria, and went about her day.

For those that don't know, Yoruba is a tonal language, with many words having the exact same spelling but with different meanings, depending on how you pronounce the word.

Not too long after, I verified with my friend what I thought happened that morning. I asked her what she thought I meant when I say "ewa".

"Beans?"

I couldn't stop laughing, and my friend couldn't stop either once I caught her up on the story.

This isn't the first time I've had communication issues with Nigerians here, and until I finally get myself to tutoring at the Yoruba language center, it won't be my last.

My cleaner dyed her hair blue shortly after that incident. Instead of complimenting her on her bold and pretty choice, I simply waved and smiled at her, and kept walking.

One day, I'm hoping I'll be able to call her style choices something other than beans. (Omeiza, 2018)

Still a closeted autistic, I spoke to my new friends often about how confusing the Yoruba language could be, and asked them if they knew of those who struggled with high context conversational styles such as Yoruba proverbs and story-telling styles using allegories. My friends told me there were some who struggled, and how many who had cognitive impairments were often weeded out of the school system long before I would be able to meet them as medical students. The reality of how cultural stigma could affect a neurodivergent individual in Nigeria upset me as it did back home, and the three of us discussed how it definitely was a phenomenon that needed to be addressed and not just talked about on both sides of the world.

Shortly after our discussion, I volunteered with my psychiatry friend and many others on mental health campaign advocacies. I quickly hyperfixated on the cause, reaching out to my US connections to help fundraise the remaining money for a phase in Nigeria's first toll-free suicide hotline. I attended several events related to ending the stigma of mental illness around the southern part of the country. The advocacy I experienced in Nigeria inspired me to create I'm Heard, a nonprofit that aims to end the stigma of mental illness in minority communities in the USA.

A few months after my birthday celebration, I told my main group of friends that I was autistic. My dental student friend and I had a particularly good discussion about the state of autism in Nigeria specifically. We devised ideas to set up advocacy initiatives for Black autistics worldwide, aspiring to one day shine as brightly as Akha's and Gerald's in their impact.

My conversation with my psychiatry friend came after my nine-month tenure in Ibadan. Through the encouragement of myself and my former intern friend at Boston, she was awarded a prestigious scholarship to study at Oxford the year after we graduated. At Oxford, she contributed to various medical doctor consultations and quotes for some of my blog posts and essays I wrote. At the next celebration I had in England, I'm pretty sure I caught her rolling her eyes and smiling when I opted to arrive in a loose fitting skirt.

Part 3
Empower ment

Chapter 9
Talking to Obama vs the School Administration

Cortez Sanchez
Waldorf, Maryland, USA

"Jeans?! But cancer is in your jeans!" little Cortez exclaimed to their mom while getting ready for the first day of kindergarten. It was a typical suburban DC dreary morning, one where only the impending rain could calm their panic. Cortez recalled that they were kicking and screaming at their mom because they learned from watching the news earlier that cancer is in one's genes. Their mother thought the misunderstanding was hilarious, and the two of them often bring the incident up to others, over 30 years later. When bringing it up, however, Cortez chooses to omit the detail that it took them a while to understand that genes in one's DNA and jean fabric were two different nouns, one being significantly more serious than the other.

"All I knew is that I had to find myself a different outfit that day," they said, the smile lines on their slim face creasing before adding, "and it also didn't help that the fiber in jeans looked like DNA strands either."

Growing up, Cortez tended to take things literally. For example, as a third grader, when they were informed to not cross the street when cars were coming on their walk home, they would wait until there weren't any cars for miles in sight. In a short five-block journey from their school to their house, they would often patiently wait up to 20 minutes to cross the street to make it home. "And sometimes not even patiently," they emphasized. "[I'd] be standing on the corner stressed out waiting as other people crossed the street. And I'm thinking like, 'Oh, they think they grown huh?'" To Cortez, all the other kids around them were breaking the law that they thought was strictly enforced on children. It took several weeks for a family friend to see them and approach their mom. When the family friend asked their mom if she was aware that Cortez was late to be home because they waited until there were no cars in the far distance, Cortez beamed, anticipating that they'd be praised for doing exactly what they were supposed to do.

Their family didn't realize that their obedience to rules was a peculiar characteristic of autistic children their age. To them, Cortez just seemed well-behaved. They always followed the rules, and they learned early in school that they were supposed to do what they were told and nothing else. They made every effort to mirror the best kid in the class until they eventually surpassed them in obedience. For example, they had sensory seeking or hypersensitive inclinations for the rain. In other words, to this day Cortez loves the way the rain smells in the air, and the way it feels on Cortez's skin. In grade school, however, they weren't permitted to go outside in the rain, and when the students were called back inside, they would be the first one at the door, sacrificing a few seconds in the rain for their obedience to the rules.

Mariajosé Paton, M.A.
Columbia, South Carolina, USA

At the University of South Carolina, Mariajosé Paton is a clinical-community psychology doctoral candidate using social justice research approaches to empowering youth with marginalized identities. After I briefly met Mariajosé at a psychology conference in Florida as undergraduate students, the two of us went on our separate career paths: she deciding to stay in academia, and me eventually deciding to part ways with the field. At our virtual meeting, I enjoyed my time reconnecting with her on her experience in graduate school.

Mariajosé at first struggled to find her place in academia, since psychology has historically had a deficit approach to understanding the health and well-being of marginalized youth. She also wanted to feel like she was contributing to a larger discussion. However, she persevered and has worked on multiple research projects that strive for health and educational equity. One of these projects included her work with the School Behavioral Health Team. Headed by Dr. Mark Weist, the mission of the School Behavioral Health Team is to promote academic and personal success by reducing barriers to learning and supporting the social, emotional, and behavioral needs of all youth and families in South Carolina. Her primary work focused on behavioral health initiatives, such as services that accommodate mental health conditions such as anxiety, and neurodivergent conditions such as autism.

"We have what's called this 'corridor of shame,'" Mariajosé said, referring to an area that splits in the center of South Carolina. Most of that area or corridor is underserved and not receiving the same type of care as areas just a couple of counties away. Additionally, Black and Brown student percentages in these counties are percentages above the national average. "[South Carolina] claims to be the pioneer of mental health services, but the majority Black schools are severely underequipped."

Like Cortez, Mariajosé has experienced her fair share of ignorance within the educational system. In grad school, her research experiences made her keenly aware that those with differing support needs could be disregarded one's whole life depending on their zip code. A bachelor's degree, master's degree or Ph.D. would not necessarily make one immune. As a woman who identified as Latina, she wanted to locate gaps to fill for future generations. Mariajosé and her team started their research with the Behavioral Health Coalition of the South Carolina Hospital Association. Her team wanted to see what school behavioral health initiatives exist, and among those, what is currently working, and what needs improvement. Mariajosé regarded this research experience as a true way to feel valued and make a difference in the lives of neurodivergent students in South Carolina. In my opinion, her work set a precedent for other states to better suit students both diagnosed and undiagnosed alike.

Cortez Sanchez
Waldorf, Maryland, USA

In elementary school, Cortez made a papier mâché art project. They wanted a good grade but were nervous that the piece wasn't their best work. "I thought the thing was ugly," they said, now 34. Their rigid mindset shifted for the first time in their life when they asked their teacher for her opinion. They wanted to figure out what they could do to improve to make the papier mâché creation acceptable to her standards, but was surprised when she repeated their question back to them and asked them if *they* liked it.

"We repeated those questions 'Do *you* like it?' 'No, do *you* like it?' back and forth for a bit. I just wanted to have a good grade, and couldn't comprehend that there were no critical steps I needed to take to improve my art. That simple question kind of just blew my mind. Like I could have my own opinions on art?" Ever since, Cortez learned to create art based on their preference and personality, rather than regurgitating what other people have made and what they think they would want to see. From that day forward, Cortez decided to, in their words: "rewrite my script." They set out on a mission to make a difference, even if it would take several years to come to pass.

As Cortez grew up, they patiently waited through DC's gray winter clouds, and clear blue summer skies to experience the late spring and early summer humidity that poured rain on their skin. On a rainy day, teenage Cortez began to eye other boys crossing the street in front of them. The DC skyline blurred in the distance, with the bright white crosswalk stripes in mocking contrast. How many steps ahead were those cute, older guys from talking to them? Many, Cortez thought, as no one yet knew about their sexuality, including themself. With that, Cortez switched their vision to the suburban trees that shadowed their mom's house. They crossed the street and turned to walk in the opposite direction as the other boys.

When *Big Bang Theory* was later on the television inside their house, their mom told them that they were similar to Sheldon from

Big Bang Theory. As the show went on, even Cortez could not deny the character resemblance. For whatever reason, their family members thought Cortez seemed rude, sometimes hilariously so, other times not so much. The writers of *Big Bang Theory* never formally stated that Sheldon Cooper was autistic, so Cortez and their family were none the wiser in understanding what the similarities could mean as some extended family started to avoid them as they grew up. Through high school, they struggled to assert their academic gifts and creativity. Their grades in school were slipping. They were concerned with their life in and out of school as they never met another teacher who reminded them to ask themself the question of what Cortez liked.

Struggling to find a term for their traits, Cortez joined their local fire department in their third year of high school. Cortez was also moonlighting at a restaurant while working at the fire department. When they were serving, a few firefighters were responding to a scene near their restaurant. One of their colleagues at the restaurant side-eyed them and challenged them to join the firefighters, as they didn't believe Cortez could be one of them. They did just that. They hyperfocused on working with their firefighter colleagues at the scene and they forgot that they were technically not working for them, but for the restaurant. The manager had to retrieve them, pulling them back to the reality of their stunned restaurant colleague.

Their double occupation experience led to a conversation with a female firefighter for them to understand how most students finance college. They took jobs at the fire department and the restaurant because they couldn't afford to go on to college. When a colleague informed them about student loans, they went on to enroll in a college across the country in Arizona.

Cortez was most at peace at the sound and feel of rain. Unlike DC, Arizona was mostly dry. They recalled how they overworked themself by trying to push through anxiety-provoking moments and situations. They scolded themself for not understanding concepts as quickly as they hoped. And as a women and gender studies major, they wanted to particularly get out of their Spanish class almost as much as they wanted to smell the brief Arizona rain. During their time with tutoring, it was suggested that Cortez be referred to the disability resource office.

Disability services quickly waived the class for them, but additional services and assessments weren't provided. While the department could have done better to understand their underlying conditions, Cortez was relieved for the brief appointment with no suggestion of follow-ups. "I was almost ashamed of using it to 'get out' [of Spanish class]," Cortez recalled. They later went on to host a radio show and had an unpaid internship in the latter half of their degree. Cortez reflected on their high school days when they thought they would never secure a job or amount to anything they wanted due to teachers over-emphasizing their inability to understand cursive or analog clocks. The missed opportunity by the college's disability service to understand their neurotype and sexuality was thus combatted with a hard-earned diploma and a fresh set of interests and desires. The Obamas, of course, would fix everything soon.

Mariajosé Paton, M.A.
Columbia, South Carolina, USA

Mariajosé found 17 initiatives across the high and low-funded region of the state. She discovered that out of many behavioral health initiatives working to support students with needs such as mental health and neurodivergence, they needed to be more engaging with each other about best practices. In her team's article "Building policy support for school mental health in South Carolina," Mariajosé and her team compiled seven themes to be implemented across the state region regarded as the "corridor of shame" of school funding and state support (Franke, Paton, & Weist, 2020).

"I did a lot of work to compile mobilization methods," Mariajose told me. Some of the themes and recommendations that her team provided included:

- Mobilization and organizing: Demonstrate the role of maternal and child health state leaders in implementing strategies to support optimal emotional well-being for adolescents and young adults.
- Collaboration: Coordinate across organizations to build an integrated early childhood data system and increase capacity to train providers on evidence-based screenings and interventions that build resilience and improve child health outcomes.
- Access: Ensure that every community member has adequate and appropriate access, locally or via telehealth, to behavioral health services. Create a new, separate task force to ensure that adequate school-based behavioral health services are available in SC schools.

When I asked her if she was surprised by the common themes, she gave a two-part answer. "In a way, I was not. I've been working with people with high needs before, like autistic and Black youth. They are very quickly labeled with something that could be carried in their school records," she said, referencing how some advocacies have to do damage control after many students of color fall through the cracks. Several of the students, like Cortez, go undiagnosed and are thus vulnerable to being labeled as "an underachiever," lacking the toolset and support system to reach their full potential.

What did surprise her, however, was how the pervasive history of racism that persisted across the school system and in her field, in general, was rarely regarded as a force to overcome. The two of us discussed the grave implications it could have on the youth of color with undiagnosed conditions.

"It would be nice if there were resources for teenage boys specifically," she added. "So many [procedures] are developed through a white cultural lens...those of color have other interests that are not addressed in these manuals....We have to get people who want to fill these gaps in terms of research." Disappointed to see that there were not great resources for black teenage boys in these regions, Mariajosé continues to study and provide clinical services for that demographic, diagnosed or not, with autism.

Mariajosé's contributions and ambitions represent a growing number of people of color entering the field of clinical psychology. In my opinion, her team's research is pioneering in breaking down achievement gaps of those of color across the nation.

Cortez Sanchez
Waldorf, Maryland, USA

Cortez loved highlighting other artists through blog posts and other mediums. When they were hosting their radio show while studying in Arizona, they wrote about creatives around the area. It hadn't occurred to them at the time that they could be a creative changemaker as well, and that their radio show already made them one. A group eventually reached out to them through email, their eyes began to open about a label that they couldn't put a name to for their life thus far. The recollection was hazy, but when Cortez looked at a specific piece of art, a mural, they became stricken. Something in the mural gave them clarity that they were nonbinary, queer, and also probably neurodivergent. They self-identified and advocated for all three groups going forward.

It didn't take long for their advocacy work to be recognized by others. They soon received a phone call from an organization called Smile asking them if they wanted to represent them at the White House. The current US president, Barack Obama, would be making a speech about repealing the "Don't Ask Don't Tell" policy. Coincidentally, the speech would occur on their 21st birthday. Delighted, Cortez jumped at the opportunity.

Cortez saw several celebrities and activists, including Jennifer Beals from *Flashdance*, who they remember to this day. But they were most starstruck by the President. The Obamas walked past them before the speech, Barack Obama first. Barack Obama said they couldn't stop and pose in order for them to have the opportunity to greet everybody. They did smile at them when they suggested that Cortez could take a selfie as they were walking by, with Barack Obama just so happening to be in the background. Cortez was ecstatic to do just that.

When Michelle Obama passed by, Cortez experienced the unexpected. "It's my birthday, Michelle!" Cortez shouted with pride. They caught Michelle Obama's attention, took a picture with her, and joked that her husband said they wouldn't take one with them. "What?" Michelle Obama said through a smile, she motioned to Barack Obama in a faux stern way. "Barack, stop and let this man take a picture with you! It's his birthday." Lacking a counterpoint, Barack Obama turned back to do just that. Later, Cortez gave a brief speech about their experience near the White House. Their family watched from home in both confusion and glee as they publicly came out as autistic for the first time.

The experience with the Obamas catapulted their self-esteem. They began to make artwork catered to neurodivergent and queer individuals, which they do to this day. Recalling their experience of disability services, they decided that they would self-identify as autistic for the time being. Mariajosé at the University of South Carolina's work would propel others like Cortez to gain self-esteem and understanding years earlier. It's all of our hope that many other individuals nationwide would have the opportunity to acquire the skill set in school to advocate among the Obamas.

As for Cortez, they stopped settling for environments that they were uncomfortable in. One example was that they stopped forcing themself to wear jeans. Not necessarily because they still thought they were cancerous, but because they simply didn't feel comfortable with the material next to their skin. They also opted to work with the lights off or dimmed when they could. But they didn't just want to avoid sensory negatives, they also wanted to lean in on their sensory pleasures. To do that, they decided to return to their DC home. To the rain.

Ujima
Oxford, England

I walked up to the starting line in the curved center lane.

"On your mark." I took a quick breath, allowing myself to feel the familiar excitement and nerves of what used to be ordinary pre-race jitters. I had no reason to be here at this moment, yet for some reason I was perfectly content to take one last lap.

Weeks ago, I entered the majestic buildings of University of Oxford to pursue a masters degree in psychological research. Everything moved so quickly after that. From starting our first class, dressing up like Hogwarts students for matriculation, and connecting with colleagues who were just as surprised as me to study at the best university in the world.

Coming from an amazing high of making lifelong friends in Nigeria during my Fulbright program, I sought to join everything that interested me. Freshers Fair was the perfect place to do so. I slowed down a bit when I passed the University Athletics table. After a bit of thought, I realized that athletics was the term that the British use to call track.

"Have you run competitively before?" the woman at the stand asked me. I nodded while eyeing the other stands. The woman's eyes lit up and through my thoughts I heard her urge me to write my name, best event and time on a sheet of paper. I did while mentally preparing myself to ignore any follow-up emails.

"Get set," the official said, starting gun in the air.

I received a very sweet email from the current captain of the team, who said all the right things. She saw that I had not run in a while, but wanted me to meet the team to see if I was interested to be a part of them. She reinforced how kind and welcoming they were, and invited me to a team pizza gathering for me to see for myself. In Virginia, Cortez went to university despite teachers and family telling him he was not mentally or financially able to. I reminded myself of him in my next action by not allowing myself to fit in boxes from my past. I would not allow how I felt with my team-mates long ago stop me from interacting with these current poten-tial teammates. I couldn't decline the idea of pizza and smiles, so I went to meet the team after class.

At the same time, I looked for ways to turn my nonprofit into a possible venture-funded endeavor. I mirrored Cortez by slowly growing into independent advocacy. I wanted to continue my col-laboration with the USA and Nigeria. I got into an incubator at Oxford and promptly found a potential co-founder named Daniel, a PhD student studying computer science at Oxford. We hacked away at strategy ideas and product market fit. That was, until I had to leave for a track meet at University of Cambridge.

Turned out, I loved the team. The captains, undergraduates who were years younger than me, were so sweet. I wondered why I once was afraid of fitting in among college athletes. I figured there was no harm in showcasing my skills. Not my running skills, but my new mental health skills. Five years after stopping my Division 1 sport, I was confident and stable enough to handle all the ups and downs that came with socializing within a close knit team.

One practice turned to another. And sure enough, I found myself on the line-up for the Oxford-Cambridge Freshers Varsity Match at least 30 pounds heavier, and 30 times happier, than I was during my last race many years ago.

"Boom!" or whatever sound a gun makes when it is fired.

We were off. Well, I was primarily off in a different direction, but not on the track. By the meet, I became engrossed in my new research project focusing on artificial intelligence aversion or acceptance within neurodivergent communities. I joined a new local church too, and became heavily involved with their weekly activities. And of course, I continued to focus on my nonprofit endeavor with my new co-founder until I began to slowly fall in love with him. Not to mention connecting with my colleagues turned friends. I wasn't nearly as cool as Cortez meeting Obama, but I certainly felt full both internally and externally.

Of course, it rained during the meet, and nearly all of the practices leading up to it. I couldn't help but remind myself that such weather was prime time for snails to grow and expand. I laughed at the distant familiarity of my growing calf cramp and the breathlessness I felt as I rounded the final bend of the 400 meters, to the chagrin of my lungs. For the first time in a while, I was excited about what laid ahead of the finish line.

Shortly after I crossed the finish line, my new coach excitedly shared with me her plans for me with the team. A couple of weeks later, when my courses, friends, and business endeavors began to compete with each other, I had to tell her I was moving on. By the end of the next year I would have married my co-founder Daniel, submitted my research thesis, pitched another business for nearly $100,000 in funding, grown even more in my faith, and still stayed close to a few teammates I met before Freshers Varsity. To my surprise, the coach didn't fight to hold me back. She simply congratulated me and wished me luck in my studies and plans for the year ahead. Like Mariajosé and Cortez discovering environments that accommodate their needs, I was both relieved and grateful.

The next chapter in this book features a mother of young boys, and a young adult around the same age I was when I was on my undergraduate team. The mother is worried for her son's future, but never stops fighting for change. The young man is charging through the stigma of autism within his culture and surroundings. If I had time to talk about myself in our interviews about my short life experience, I would have advised them to never judge the future by their present. I would have told them to take each day in strides. Each morning when the gun goes off, it's important to keep racing. And if you temporarily slow down or fall at some point, get up and keep racing until you reach your own unique finish line.

Chapter 10
Nicknames
for Stigma

Nigeria • Virginia, USA

Gift
Nigeria

His nickname was "Drug Addict." A few months into the maritime academy, Gift felt he was finally becoming what his dad expected of him. Growing up in one of Nigeria's largest cities, he was scolded for being disorganized. Gift's scolding continued in the military academy, except to a greater degree with beatings and shouting. Promptly, he was forced to straighten up both himself and his living space.

The sergeants, others in command, and even his peers in the academy would make fun of him for forgetting key instructions. After a few misplaced boots, forgotten chores, and forgetting the paths of some training courses, those around him began to lose patience. It was surprising to those around them that he was not able to comprehend what seemed to be simple tasks. For Gift, it was just another day of an otherwise upward progression.

Gift traded in the hustle and bustle of his large city for a relatively more lush, quieter dwelling in a smaller town where the maritime academy was located. He recalled his mind being just as cluttered as it was in his home city. For one, he was sometimes so overwhelmed with his surroundings that he became overstimulated.

"Kú iṣẹ́" or "well done" is what he probably mumbled to his brother when he paused to take a breath. Gift was visiting his brother's apartment and watched as he cooked a Yoruba soup delicacy called efo riro. His brother was speaking about something that, in Gift's words, "was not particularly interesting." The spicy aroma of onions, broth and the various array of seasonings and meat smelled delicious yet overbearing. Gift recalled how his brother was making a joke and leaned in for the punchline, and Gift flinched because he assumed he would touch him.

"Please do not touch me!" Gift yelped in irritation, making his brother stumble backwards. Looking back, Gift recalled to me how it was just one of many early examples of how he had gotten overstimulated by too many senses at once. The occurrence is now a running joke between the two brothers, with the older one teasing Gift with tempting offers such as "Are you going to pay me not to touch you this time?"

Gift clearly isn't fond of physical touch being combined with the smell of delicious food, and chattering. However, he also struggled with keeping up in school, a dilemma that was evident in both grade school and the maritime academy. In school, Gift was known to have several niche interests that he would go in and out of, such as science fiction, anime, and, most recently, autism. As a single parent, his dad was often irritated at how he seemed to be focused on everything except the task at hand. Gift came home from primary and secondary school with empty notebooks and a head full of daydreams and interesting facts outside of the primary subjects. "I was seen as a smart kid with bad grades," Gift said, remembering how he sat next to his friend who wrote prolific notes. The friend often came to him for answers on topics, but it was always that friend who came out with the highest grade at the end of the term.

There weren't special education services or even disability professionals in the public schools of most of his home city when Gift was growing up. To this day, it is commonplace for teachers and other staff members to flog or beat unruly students. Additionally, most homes in Nigeria are religious in some way (Pardung & Chukwuemeka, 2023). Many parents are obedient to religious texts that state that children need to be disciplined by beatings as well. If a student is particularly unruly or receiving consistently poor grades, it is not uncommon for attentive parents to turn to churches, mosques, ritualists, or other means for prayer, exhortation, herbs, or the religious equivalent. Most adult figures consult these sources not only because the sources are valued and respected, but also because those were often the only resources that they had, as there were not any alternatives. When there are, a lot of teachers and parents in charge of public school youth are unaware.

While there are disparities regarding lack of resources like the above in the USA and other Western nations, they are exacerbated in the developing world, where nearly all neurodiverse youth go undiagnosed. My psychiatry friend from my Fulbright endeavor, Rhodes Scholar Boluwatife Ikwunne, M.D., had the following to say about the lack of autism diagnosis among Nigerians—where psychiatrists are just 300 strong among a population of over 200 million (Ogunyemi, 2022).

In Nigeria, autism is often undiagnosed and left unmanaged. This is largely due to poor awareness, a lack of screening tools and unavailable/inaccessible supportive facilities. A national policy on neurodevelopmental disorders does not exist, meaning that neurodiverse students do not have access to reasonable accommodation facilities or other inclusive measures to aid learning and improve their quality of life. (Boluwatife Ikwunne, in Omeiza, 2021)

Many students, such as the Nigerian students Dr. Ikwunne mentioned, may not be able to receive accommodation for a disability simply because they and their community are not aware that said disability exists (Omeiza, 2021). Alternatively, when the student grows up in the digital world they may read about some neurodivergent symptoms, or even stumble upon an autism forum or two. Still, there is not much to do with such information, as the stigma and shame faced by one's immediate community would be too harsh. That was exactly the case with Gift in both his home city and new smaller town in Nigeria.

During the academy, Gift stumbled across blog posts that discussed sensory likes and dislikes such as the one that he had. He found a program where uncertified individuals evaluated those curious in his home city. He was surprised when they suggested he get a referral for an official diagnosis. It was validating that his initial gut feeling about his similarity to Western autistics could be confirmed. Gift declined to go for a real diagnosis for several reasons. One, both the wait and cost of obtaining a diagnosis were too high due to the scarcity of qualified professionals, as Dr. Ikwunne stated earlier. The rare psychiatrists who do conduct official assessments and are qualified to provide diagnosis often prioritize nonspeakers or those whose family members considered them to be "severely disabled."

"It's crazy expensive," Gift emphasized, "and my health insurance wasn't covering that." He decided to self-diagnose as autistic with the information he had. When he returned home from the academy on break, he took a large inhale as he explained to his family his new identity, and a foreign terminology.

Gift's father was a bit perplexed. Not surprising, considering he witnessed Gift grow up with difficulties in school and scolded him accordingly.

"I would never forget this crazy look my dad would give me when I was just staring away one time," Gift reflected. He was staring at a television that was turned off for a long period that he can't recall enough to quantify. His dad walked in, looked at the TV, looked at Gift, and looked in a mix of incredulity and bewilderment. "It was almost like [my dad thought] I was needing some sort of church deliverance." A spirituality conversation wouldn't be the first time to make an appearance in his household, as his dad, tutor and sometimes brother deemed his neurodivergent symptoms equivalent to a spiritual problem.

As for Gift's half-brother? Well, he gave a similar reaction, but was also able to voice his. "He said he always knew that there was something weird about me," Gift said while smiling. Gift recalled he and his brother's running joke about him not wanting to be touched, and wondered how much more would have made sense to them all if he had discovered the meaning of neurodivergent sooner. How would his family react if Nigeria had a healthcare system that accommodated official autism diagnosis? How would his school experience be different had he been in an environment that accepted his difference? While Gift enjoys pondering those questions on African autism forums, he had no time to think along those lines during his short break in the academy.

Before he knew it, Gift's short break came to an end and he had to return to the smaller town. At the academy, surrounded by lush greenery and a population that was less in a rush than in his home city, he put his mask back on. For him, the academy has been a positive experience, as he told me he enjoyed his sense of regimentation. He hustled to keep up with the other cadets. He tried his best to avoid being called his "Drug Addict" nickname, shortening the frequency to not too often. Once, the sergeant came in one morning, and Gift's bed was made, the floor swept, and all other chores completed.

"Kú iṣẹ́," was the compliment. Although Gift can't quite recall if the sergeant had told him well done, or if he had, while daydreaming, said the phrase to himself.

Meghan Ashburn
Virginia, USA

Her nickname was "not an autism mom," and for a good reason. On the United States East Coastline, Meghan realized her children were going to be as unique as Virginia Beach's four seasons. She and her husband are raising four boys, with their youngest twins diagnosed with autism. They found out about the condition when one of the twins, Jay, was diagnosed primarily because he is non-speaking. Meghan's second twin, Nick, was originally misdiagnosed. "They thought he had an intellectual disability, which was definitely not true," Meghan told me. Fortunately, Nick was able to receive his official diagnosis by five.

Nick grew up to be very protective of his twin brother, and often suffered the consequences of standing up to authority when he was small. One day when the twins were in preschool, Meghan gasped when she saw Nick come off the bus bloodied.

"He had a hard day," was all the bus driver said. Meghan promptly called the school and learned that Nick didn't finish his work on time during the day. As a punishment, he was not allowed to go outside to play. Unable to help defend his twin brother from bullies, Nick started scratching himself in anguish until he bled.

Meghan, a white woman, knew what life would likely be like for her Black sons. She grew up in a diverse neighborhood, and saw how her Black friends and classmates were treated growing up. She has also always listened to her Black husband's recollections and read more information on her own about topics such as racism and microaggression. Still, the treatment of her twins, especially Jay, felt different. She didn't like how Jay was being excluded to the extent that Nick put himself in pain for the chance to protect his twin. The behavior she received from the school was different from the school's behavior with her two oldest sons. They entered high school as typical, popular kids. In a diverse school system, like their mom's formative years, they had enough representation in the school to never feel particularly outcast. The distinct differences between the two sets of brothers made her scratch her head.

While Meghan put in the work to understand racial prejudices, she found that she was lacking in the space of understanding disability prejudices. It didn't help that Nick wasn't officially diagnosed until kindergarten. The delay in her sons' diagnosis bothered her as well, and she wasn't alone.

As stated previously in this book, Black children are often diagnosed with autism spectrum disorder later than their white peers. These Black children are often more likely to be misdiagnosed, and less likely to receive early intervention by age three. Often these occurrences occur when the Black child is not necessarily showing "obvious" signs such as being nonspeaking (Dababnah et al., 2018).

Such was the case with Meghan's son Nick. What's interesting about these phenomena that Meghan shared is how such racial biases overrode statistics and medical facts.

Racial bias and stereotypes that practitioners have about autism are one way that can limit diagnosis and access to services. But an outstanding occurence of this is how these negative thought processes occur even with other scientific evidence to look at. For example, a meta-analysis published by Cambridge University Press showed that a twin is significantly more likely to be diagnosed with autism if the other twin already has a diagnosis (Gardener, Spiegelman, & Buka, 2009). Why then was Nick overlooked, misdiagnosed at first, and then diagnosed later than the age of three?

Meghan's suspicion reminded her of the differences of privileges she as a white woman had with her Black friends, classmates, and family up until the present time. The academic in me wanted to do my own investigating. While looking further into the meta-analysis, it was clear that the original studies that formed this data were conducted from 1995 to 2006, including the highly cited British twin study from 1995 (Bailey et al., 1995; Klauck, 2006; Neschaffer, Fallin, & Lee, 2002; Santangelo & Tsatsanis, 2005) Turns out, Meghan's theory was correct: that racism is what overruled what most modern-day practitioners would have been taught about twins.

From my aforementioned personal experience befriending and working with researchers, doctors, and psychologists, it is not surprising to me that bias played a factor. It is understandable for professionals to be blinded by personal relationships of those with undiagnosed conditions. I also understand and appreciate how I too, as a budding researcher, was at one point guilty of seeing only what I wanted to see about autism: a nonspeaking, violent (over-stimulated) white toddler, and not making an effort to think about the ramifications of that thinking, and of course not considering alternative perspectives. What's more, several researchers and clinicians still treat autism as a disorder worth eliminating, which propagates the stigma of well-meaning professionals learning about the condition and relaying news to their patients. Regardless, the consistent stigma I faced surrounding what were factual signs and signals of autism in myself and those like me eventually made me skeptical and made it difficult for me to trust professionals in the future. Thankfully (yet unfortunately that she had to) Meghan felt the same. Meghan turned to other resources for ways to assist her sons.

As with most parents, Meghan and her husband wanted the best for their children, and she strived to find a way to create an equitable outcome for her autistic twins. While most researchers focus on causes for autism, Meghan looked for advocacy initiatives, online forums, or anything that could help her give her children the happy and comfortable life they deserved. Turns out, the stigma propagated by professionals was also relayed by parents. She looked on in horror at the term "autism mom" beginning to form and increasingly gain global traction.

Meghan was tired of the treatment that she was receiving from professionals who were meant to protect her and her family. "[The treatment hurts in] so many different ways," she told me. "One year [Jay] had a teacher who would basically trigger him or taunt him. Or treat him as if he was like an animal. She would send him home…, [in school] he would stand on tables, chairs, [she] would depict him as animalistic." When Meghan turned to the "autism mom" groups, she was horrified to find that most of the parents blamed either themselves or their child for such behavior. For her, it was clearly a problem with the system, and those not adapting to her child's differences.

"But, it's like, [the first twin Jay] doesn't do that at home? He damn sure does not stand on my tables," she told me while shaking her head. She rested her elbow on her desk and covered her mouth with her hands at the memory. "They spoke about him as if he was some out of control person...but he's six? Why is it always his fault?" Meghan tried to gather more "autism moms" to her opinion that the school structure might not be best at accommodating both her twins and other children like them. Unfortunately, Meghan's voice was often silenced by those who posted videos of their child's most vulnerable moments during a meltdown. She also competed with various posts of parents victimizing themselves and claiming how they were, to summarize, "winning the battle of autism". Meghan knew how bright and beautiful her twins' personalities were. After having two neurotypical sons just a few years older, it upset her that one condition could stigmatize her just as capable twins for life. Fortunately, Meghan's diverse upbringing was not a coincidence. Her mother was an advocate for change in all parts of society, and Meghan knew that it was time to formally follow in her mom's footsteps.

"I feel like my mom prepared me for my kids," Meghan said, while beaming. She told me how her mother has always been service and activist minded. For one, her mother founded the Early Head Start Program in their hometown. The program benefits low-income mothers to get the help they need through pregnancy and until their child is three years old. She also founded a children's center and various initiatives that benefitted Black and Brown families specifically.

"She was always focused on what's right, what's equitable. My mom showed me how to advocate and how to navigate," Meghan continued. When I asked her how her childhood of advocacy formed her future brand, she said, "[My mom's] example had me thinking about how we can make sure that other people can access services that are accessible to everyone. It was the mindset that she had... she did prepare me for that."

Meghan didn't fit in with the other "autism mom" groups, and neither did she want to. She utilized one of her mom's favorite sayings, "It doesn't matter what's popular, it matters what's right," and took action. At first, Meghan started local. Her sons were registered in the Individualized Education Program for all children that were diagnosed with having a special needs condition such as autism. Meghan voiced her concern at an Individualized Education Program Meeting where many practitioners and "autism moms" whose children had negative interactions with some practitioners were gathered. "I think I got somebody fired that day," she said through a grin. Meghan told me how she informed the members and parents that children need to be treated as unique individuals, and autistic children specifically should not be treated like children that needed to be tamed. She spoke out about the ramifications for her children and others that were recipients of the Individualized Education Program, and being tracked for life for having meltdowns due to overstimulation or mismanagement of accommodations. "Like there's a record of [Nick] being a violent person," she told me, "when he's never violent, [the teacher was] just a bitch."

Meghan increasingly expanded her advocacy outside of her school system. She became a content creator on social media and took on the name "Not an Autism Mom." Curiosity from autistic individuals, autism researchers, practitioners, and "autism moms" grew, and she later opened a virtual book club for each group to come together and learn more through autistic authors. Day by day, her reach continued to grow, and she found herself a part of national conversions pertaining to race, disabilities, and social justice at large. Not bad for *not* an autism mom.

Their nicknames were "advocates." Both Gift and Meghan grew into themselves in locations where stigma of autism and general neurodivergence were high. From his computer in Nigeria, Gift began speaking out about being a neurodivergent individual in his country. He joined the Autism in Africa network, where he grew in popularity by discussing ways for better self-advocacy across the continent. In North America, Meghan admired the work that those on the African continent were accomplishing. She spoke to me about how she interviewed Danny With Words in her book club. Danny is a popular nonspeaking Asian American who didn't learn how to use the popular spell to communicate program until he was in his thirties. Referencing children like Ndomi and Akha, the children from South Africa who were featured in parts one and two of this book respectively, Meghan wished that the program was better implemented in communities of color in the USA as well.

On both sides of the world, their nicknames continue to evolve. Gift continues to shed his nickname of "Drug Addict," online at least, as he's found community and purpose in connecting with others like himself across Nigeria and the African continent. Meghan has been delighted to witness others also disassociating themselves with the stereotypical "autism mom" mentality. She has relished seeing her twin boys and others she has connected with through social media grow to become confident youth and young adults. The phrase "Not an Autism Mom" has grown as the overall stigma of autism during childhood has shrunk. However, like all advocacies, there is still plenty of work to be done.

In Nigeria, for example, there is still a scarcity of psychiatrists and other practitioners who can help formally diagnose children like Gift. The state of the Nigerian economy has made it imperative for those like my colleague Dr. Ikwunne to move elsewhere for better safety and stability. This "brain-drain" means that there must be focused work by both Nigerians and those in the diaspora to advocate for change at home. In the USA, more advocates like Meghan are needed to utilize their privilege of any kind, and work to create a better world for all. Injustices still happen to Black and autistic youth specifically on both Gift's side of the world and Meghan's. For example, my interview with Meghan was interrupted by a phone call from school. She put her face in her hands in frustration as she told me that one of her sons had just been suspended. Ready to fight for fairness among all races in the school system, and serve as her child's advocate for now, she postponed the second half of our interview, and got back to work.

Ujima
Oxford, England • Oxford, Ohio, USA

"How were you able to overcome loneliness here?" a young woman with an impressive afro who was seated near me at Miami University asked. Several others came up to me during my book signing event, making comments and asking questions like "You're so inspiring...how did you know you were autistic?" and "How were you able to accomplish so much after graduating?" I smiled at them, in awe at how so many of the young men and women looked like me a few years ago, and inspired that, unlike me, they had the courage and understanding to come to an event such as this. I thought about the courage that Meghan and Gift (who I had already spoken to at that time) had as they advocated for their needs and accommodation for family. I was grateful that others like Meghan and Gift were utilizing the power of the internet to locate and connect with those who might have more insight. And these Miami students looked at me. I did not feel qualified to have all the answers, but I did my best to give the best advice I could.

The years following my Oxford graduation, I received an alumni award from Miami University for those who had graduated in the last nine years. Stephanie Dawson, the current director of Disability Services, and I had been communicating about doing outreach activities for those who were undiagnosed with disabilities and/or neurodivergent conditions. We enjoyed brainstorming several ideas, including a campus wide art project, and various initiatives for those in minority-led student organizations. When Stephanie and her department invited me back to campus to give a keynote address for their annual disability and cultures month, I was thrilled. I had not been back to the USA in three years by that point, and it was over six years since I last walked the hiking trails or hung out with Allyson or other college friends in Ohio.

The experience encompassed my first ever formal book signing event. My debut novel, *Afrotistic*, was recently published by the time I visited campus. The novel, featuring 15-year-old Noa, was the first of its kind to feature a Black autistic female. The discussion and signing event left me in awe of the curious fresh set of students before me. I discussed with the group of students around me a similar comment I made in my keynote later that evening:

"As a Black autistic woman, who didn't consider that autism could apply to me, I labeled myself as many things, and other people helped as well. I was anti-social. I was bougie. I was weird, awkward, obsessed, etc. etc. I called myself helpless before ever feeling hopeful. I called myself lazy before I called myself loved. I would be sitting at a large dining table at Brandon Hall's cafeteria, surrounded by other Black athletes and smart ambitious students, and feeling completely alone."

The students at my book event were mostly of color. Rather than wanting to hear more about why I felt the way I did (as I imagined they already understood), they asked me how I was able to blossom in my upper years in undergrad and the years after. For me, I attributed it to a term I coined called the Hedonic Flywheel Effect. While I worked to scale up various start-ups, I developed the term by combining two theories: the Hedonic Treadmill (a theory that shows that people return to their original baseline of happiness or sadness shortly after a distinctive life event occurs) and the Flywheel Effect (building consistent momentum rather than relying on one great push to achieve success). When I read more about the Flywheel Effect, and how business leaders such as Jeff Bezos implemented that strategy to succeed at Amazon, I reflected on my life to that point in how the positive (hedonic) momentum (flywheel) led to improvements not only in my career, but within my friendships, and relationships.

"It took me a few years to reflect on how trying new things to discover different interests and talents would go on to serve me well in the future," I said in my keynote.

> ...This is actually what I call the hedonic flywheel effect. It's a term I completely made up, but I use it to describe two things; how

being happy in your ambition, and surrounding yourself with happy ambitious people can spiral into unanticipated success and even greater joy. Also, how putting yourself out there occasionally is such a crucial investment in that it allows yourself to discover new interests and talents. Once you cultivate your interests further, you find that opportunities start to pop up, as well as even like-minded friends. It keeps spinning into what is considered a flywheel.

I talked about how, after my suicide attempt at Miami, I pivoted from track to volunteering in my community, better connected with my faith, and participated in academic research. I found that I was able to make like-minded friends in all of those domains, who were then able to introduce me to other friends and other fun interests, which kept expanding like a flywheel. I talked about how I was able to meet people like Allyson and Stephanie Dawson while breaking free and following my passions wherever they led. Some of the best friends and colleagues I met led to exponential increase in my happiness and fulfillment, continuing the cycle. After the presentation, for example, Allyson gave me another blanket that she knitted just for me, encouraging me to keep persevering.

The crowd giggled at how I described my interest in mental health, Nigeria, and business at the time led me to not only amazing career opportunities and great friends, but also my husband. If it interests you, I encourage you to look up the Hedonic Flywheel Effect and its application on my life and others featured in this book on my website.

In the next and final chapter of this book, I talked to two individuals who had similar feelings of isolation. Both of these individuals had several hurdles in front of them before ultimately finding value in work, friendship, and even romantic relationships. Maria and Rawiya, featured next, along with several others in the book, embody the Hedonic Flywheel Effect to perfection.

Chapter 11
Connected and Unmasked

Rawiya Gadine
Near the West Virginia/Virginia border, USA

Just like Olivia in Chapter 1, a woman with the alias Rawiya came to the virtual meeting exactly on time. She briefly stated how she was from a town near the border with the US Appalachian region. However, just like Olivia and I, Rawiya and I tried to stick to our usual conversational script. Both mirroring each other's smiles and facial expressions. Both making an effort to reframe from blinking, fidgeting, touching our hair, face or arms. I wish I could say that I have fully adapted to unmasking with others in my culture, but I found the urge instinctual still. Rawiya was very pretty, and had a resting face in a way that made me wonder if I was being judged. I oh so wanted to keep mirroring her facial expression, as it was something that I have learned to do to be accepted in nearly every location that I'm in. Fortunately, right before my rehearsed script about the book project and the purpose of our interview, I, again, saw the light.

What if Rawiya is masking just like me?, I thought. If I keep my guard up with her and mask, wouldn't that mean I'm misjudging her? And how would that make me any different than people in the past who misjudged me?

I didn't want Rawiya to hold back on sharing her life with me, and most importantly, I didn't want her to miss out on connecting with a fellow Black autistic woman in the way that we should have been accepted for long before this meeting. I'm sure she had an amazing story of overcoming her past and advocating for a better future. Odds were, she had as much to say as everybody else I interviewed, and—like me—just needed to unmask.

"Appalachia?" I asked while taking a few satisfying blinks. "How was it like growing up there with your family?"

Rawiya looked to the side and shrugged. "Not great," she said. Then, in all meanings of the phrase, we both leaned in.

Rawiya faced physical and emotional abuse during the majority of her childhood. Her parents were in their seventies, and Rawiya knew from an early age that they treated her brother kinder than her. She couldn't quite pinpoint why when she was a toddler emerging to school age. She did not have a reference for her half-sister who was over 30 years older than her, as she was just too far into adulthood to engage with Rawiya much. Rawiya's brother, however, was only a bit over a year older than she was, yet everything he did seemed to be correct, while everything she did seemed to be wrong.

"It felt like my parents didn't really care much about me," she said. "When we go to church they would call [my brother] 'professor.' My parents would have the congregants only focus on how pretty I was and things like that." She rolled her eyes when telling me how her parents didn't try to stop the patriarchal comments, but encouraged them. "[Everyone at church] would talk to me like I was stupid. Not because of autism, but because I was a little girl, and not as smart as boys." Unfortunately, Rawiya was also subjected to physical abuse that lasted the majority of her childhood. All of this traumatized her, and eventually made her want to do everything possible to prevent it from happening to others.

Rawiya was lucky to have some respite while in school. She recalls crossing paths with another six-year-old at the time with similar life experience at an innocent age. "She told me how something awful happened when she was on a vacation with one of her parents," Rawiya said, "And I shared something that was happening in my home life." Since then, the two have made an effort to get to know each other better and look out for each other. They would grow up to become teenagers who would band together in failed attempts to convince their parents to take them to the mall and buy anything their hearts desired. Her friendship with this girl would later become a lifeline as Rawiya grew into adulthood.

One of the most traumatizing occurrences to happen to Rawiya was in the summer before 6th grade. She was supposed to read four summer reading books before she resumed school. Near the end of the summer, her dad found out that she forgot to complete the fourth book. Rawiya blinked heavily as she told me that her dad began to strangle her with his hands when he confronted her.

"All over a book!" Rawiya told me. She felt that her dad was trying to severely harm her. Her saving grace was when her mom and brother stormed into her room, looked at ten-year-old Rawiya's father, and the brother shouted "If you don't stop, I'm going to kill you."

Rawiya emphasized how she had undiagnosed dyslexia. Unfortunately, struggling to keep up in reading and other subjects compared to her peers was exacerbated by the fact that her brother was hyperlexic and could read before his second birthday. Rawiya remembers completing her spelling homework one night, looking out of the window alone in the dining room in front of the Christmas tree, eyeing a fuchsia Christmas ornament in particular. She looked at her reflection in the nearby window, then again at the Christmas ornament, telling herself that she'd never learn how to read or communicate appropriately. Looking at her reflection once again, she was saddened about what she just spoke about herself at such a young age. Rawiya broke into tears when she told me how she had her first thoughts of harming herself at that time.

Her experiences at home and during grade school were what kept her from forming romantic relationships through college. She felt that no one explained the difference between romantic attraction and sexual attraction. The concept made her question her own sexuality, wavering between identifying as asexual or demisexual. However, unlike her brother, Rawiya has an eidetic memory. While it means that she wouldn't be able to forget her traumatic experiences, she would later be able to work through them and find a way to move forward. One example of her stark memory needing to heal was her experiencing one year of housing insecurity as a child. She is grateful for the experience she has had in therapy to help her to achieve healing-transformation that will later conclude this chapter and the last featured section in the book.

Over the years, Rawiya would begin to make peace with her family and herself. It would take several years of healing during a period that she described as "Confusing, 'volatile', abusive, dark, and sad." Soon, though, Rawiya would start to fight back ethically. She would stand up not only for herself, but others around her. I, for one, smiled when she described a similar timeline of events as mine when I celebrated a mid-decade birthday in Ibadan, Nigeria. Rawiya mirrored my smile and continued. Soon, she would turn her situation around for good. Soon, Rawiya would turn 25.

Maria Davis Pierre
Florida, USA

For Maria, family is everything. Her husband, for example, is her one and only true love. In her office in her sunny Florida home, Maria described to me how their opposite personalities make them best friends. "He's very patient, very easygoing and relaxed," she said, noting that it's what makes him more empathetic to her needs. She proudly told me how he understands a lot of her deficits, and she understands his. The two of them work together to pick up the slack for the other.

For Maria, her husband was a once-in-a-lifetime match. She noticed during most of her twenties and early thirties that many individuals perceived her to be uninterested in them. Often, those she wanted to get close to were confused when Maria would sometimes not want to be around them. She didn't like talking on the phone, and certainly had a low threshold of tolerance when communicating in person. Friends and some family grew distant from her, frustrated at the amount of one-sided effort it took to pursue and maintain their relationship. Maria's husband, on the other hand, loved being around everybody, to use her words. "His personality allows him to be me in front of anyone," she added. "He's the only one that knows me at my most vulnerable, naked state, he knows 100 percent of who I am."

Maria's husband has known her since she was 21. For that reason, coupled with their deep bond, it made sense to hear that he wasn't at all surprised that his wife was diagnosed with autism spectrum disorder at the age of 38.

Among the palm trees and warm Florida nature, Maria noticed similarities between herself and her first daughter. For one, her daughter had specific sensory issues that she could relate to.

"The grass in the backyard was not okay, but the grass in the front yard was okay," Maria said about her daughter, now in grade school, with a smile. As a baby, Maria was also attentive that her daughter had a slower reaction time to respond to her name compared to other babies she knew. As a therapist and married to a physician, she grew attentive to her baby girl's reaction times and other symptoms, and decided to have her see a professional which led to her daughter being diagnosed with autism at 18 months.

Ever since Maria's oldest daughter was diagnosed, she did everything in her power to make sure she had a childhood that was safe and accommodating for her. She and her husband did not force her to eat foods that their daughter was not interested in. Thankfully, due to Florida's diverse greenery, they were also able to accommodate the type of parks and fields that she felt most comfortable playing in. "My thing is to protect [my daughter], and protect them all as much as possible. I don't want her or any of our children to be traumatized," Maria said, as she later had twins, one boy and one girl. The girl was later diagnosed with ADHD, and the boy was diagnosed with autism as well.

Maria and her husband advocated for their children while often keeping in mind that they were at a more privileged vantage point compared to their peers.

"Our educational background had all kinds of merit," Maria said, listing the financial privileges it afforded their family, followed by the flexibility and time. "And that was just one test!" In the school system, the couple found that they had to consistently advocate for their children to have the services and respect they deserve.

"In my daughter's experience…once they find out she is autistic… she gets the 'infantilization' portion," Maria said as she put a finger of one hand to the palm of the other. She said she felt that because her daughter was quiet with her condition, she wasn't seen as smart as her other peers. "[The school] tried to get her in the non-diploma track…and she's in first grade! Makes no sense."

"And with the boys," Maria added, as she put a second finger of one hand to the palm of the other, "I see a lot of Black [autistic] boys who have behavioral issues. When they have a diagnosis, they only focus on their behavior, and put them on the school-to-prison pipeline."

Thanks to her flexibility with time off from work, Maria was able to attend various school board and parent–teacher association meetings to advocate for all three of her children. Also, due to the good and more well-funded school district they were in, the staff had more time and resources to allocate to her. She slowly started to see even more of herself in her children, which she appreciated for the onset of self-discovery. Still, Maria became angry about this, as she was aware that not all Black people were allowed similar privileges. Due to redlining and other racist housing practices, she knew it was a rare occurrence for Black people to have the advantages that she was afforded in her life.

"And what about the Black parents that don't have this privilege?" she thought, and that's when she formed the organization "Autism in Black." "I formed Autism in Black out of that desperation, under that anger, under that frustration. [The healthcare system] is not explaining everything, and then they want to get mad that we don't know."

Maria founded Autism in Black in the months leading up to receiving her official diagnosis. She was very proud of her work and enjoyed a deep sense of fulfillment with the organization. Most specifically, she felt most fulfilled with catering to the specific needs of Black families like hers. She felt that the majority of training, such as catering to parents of autistic children, was primarily led by white individuals who did not understand the particular needs of Black children, let alone how their race intersected with autism.

"I only have Black parents [clients]. Or white parents who have black children," Maria said, because of the name of the organization, and how we speak about our experiences and our culture, they have let their guard down and tell me 'you get it.'" Her fondest memory with a client was how she was able to work with a fellow mother of autistic children. On the family's behalf, Maria advocated for that child. She noticed that there was a knowledge gap between her and some of the staff at the school regarding how to treat autistic children in general, most likely due to a lack of funding. When the staff accepted Maria's terms on behalf of the family, the child's mother was relieved to have someone step in for her. However, while she experienced personal fulfillment with her clients, she was also taken aback by the feedback she received outside of the organization.

Maria leaned back in her chair as she recalled all of the harassment and racism she received from people who saw her organization's social media accounts. She told me that some were sending her pictures of gorillas, baboons, and monkeys in response to seeing an organization catered toward Black people.

"It's because of the name," she said with a shrug, "it scares a lot of racist people. Every year we advertise the conference. I get racists." When I asked her about those who thought the organization was a case of identity politics, or used the term against her, she said she brushed them off and told me "I did not invent racism or that gap. If there were organizations like what I was doing, I wouldn't do it. Black families and Black people are getting harmed, hurt and left behind. I'd always rather deal with the racists and trolls being left behind." Fortunately, those that were out to tear her down were overshadowed by those who were enthusiastic about amplifying the organization.

The encouragement she received was also unexpected but gratifying for Maria as Autism in Black began to get off the ground. She leaned forward in her chair and enthusiastically attributed the applause to her organization's name. "Also because of the name, the name is bold. I will never apologize for talking about Black people specifically. Everything I do is detailed to the Black experience. Our community needed that." Before she knew it, high-profile people and media outlets were interviewing her during the peak of the Black Lives Matter media attention. She noted that it slightly trickled down after 2020, but unlike organizations and initiatives led by others I interviewed, she was relieved to see that the overall interest and attention didn't waver too much.

Maria credits her husband and children for the work that she does. Her husband, a physician, was both inspired and encouraged by her work. He often talked to her about how there isn't specific training in how to communicate and accommodate autistic individuals. After partnering with Maria and Autism in Black, he is hopeful about seeing a change in diagnosis and treatments in the Black autistic community. Maria's family happily embraced her when she came home with her autism diagnosis in 2022. With the loving approval of her family, Maria continues to actively look out for others in her community in order for others to—one day—receive the accommodation and respect they deserve from society.

Rawiya Gadine
Near the West Virginia/Virgina border, USA

In her words, Rawiya struggled through the rest of grade school in her town. After later graduating from college, she felt deep down that something was not quite right. Rawiya identifies as being on the asexual spectrum, specifically demisexual. She often does not want to have a sexual relationship with others, and if she does, she doesn't want to until there's at least an emotional connection. While she experienced plenty of emotional connections through college and shortly after, she struggled to maintain romantic relationships, and platonic relationships to a lesser extent.

Confused with the dearth of safe romantic partners she had, she sought the services of a family therapist. She was grateful that the psychologists she had from later in college and beyond had been accommodating to her needs, primarily by being direct and straight-forward. With the use of therapy, she was able to focus on what she enjoyed most. She cultivated her version of the Hedonic Flywheel Effect and was intentional about discovering more about her major in environmental science. She was passionate about learning about the effects that climate change has had on the planet, and the various strategies scientists and world leaders have proposed to do less harm. Rawiya's dedication to her interest in climate change mirrored Maria's with her children. Additionally, Rawiya resembled my own Hedonic Flywheel Effect journey in how she pivoted her interests and her goals when she could, both by enhancing her talents and taking care of the parts of herself that needed to grow.

Rawiya continued to cultivate her interests through the unpleasant moments of her adult years. Someone who she thought was a great friend of hers cut off all contact after months of connection. To this day, Rawiya doesn't quite understand why she was ghosted. While the experience stunned her for a bit, she didn't let it stop her interest in climate change. Around that time she became a content creator for the topic and started posting videos and infographics on social media. She was happy to see her followership amass, and connect with others online as they bonded over a shared interest. Thanks to her becoming more aware of herself with the help of a therapist, Rawiya has been able to manage the account and the connections it brought well. "I now learned to better regulate my emotions," Rawiya told me, both of us smiling with pride. "It was hard to access that because of my upbringing, but it's here now."

Fortunately, Rawiya was still in contact with her childhood friend she met when she was just six years old. In recent times the two of them primarily get together during the holidays as the friend is studying outside of the country. When the next holiday period came, the two of them finally went to cross-off their teenage bucket list item of going to the mall.

"We wanted to get perfume," Rawiya said. "It was funny because we were so similar, especially with our smell preferences. We're basically the same person. It's neat watching each other grow up over the years." Rawiya maintaining a relationship with her childhood friend throughout the years is similar to Maria's relationship with her husband. Through trials and tribulations, both pairs were able to have at least one person they could rely on to be good to them, and who they would be good to.

Rawiya also started to pivot her interest to autism and how it intersected with both her race and other disabilities. She discussed her experience of being diagnosed and living with autism on her social media account as well. Gradually, her followers began to adjust, and most loved hearing her perspective on the two important topics of climate change and disability rights.

I noticed Rawiya's posture appeared more confident as she talked about therapy, how she cultivated her interests, and how she grew to trust others again. Her eidetic memory, she noted, was no longer used to look at the past in spite, but in the future with hope. I also noticed how she stopped mirroring my mannerisms as our interview progressed... Or maybe it was me who stopped mirroring hers. Either way, I was inspired by and happy to hear how she overcame significant hurdles in her childhood, and misunderstandings in relationships to cultivate new and better connections.

However, with the help of her therapist, new burgeoning real-life platonic friendships, and the fun she's experienced with her interests on her social media page, Rawiya was able to begin the process of moving on. She did have work to do, after all. She had herself as an autistic person to advocate for, much more a vulnerable population affected by climate change. However, the first thing was first, and I noticed my eyes light up in recognition as she told me about her last significant outreach. Unmasked too, I let my eyes dart around the room as they probably flickered in recognition as Rawiya described to me the connections she's made during her last engagement. Like my keynote and book talk event at Miami, Rawiya described her friendly and refreshing speaking engagement where she was able to meet others, often younger than her, who needed to hear her story.

Ujima
Nairobi, Kenya

A few days before my 29th birthday, I found myself back in Kenya, unemployed and briefly resentful. My husband's friends and he created a start-up the year prior that set out to help mend the poor credit infrastructure across Africa.

Fast forward several months, and the four of us found ourselves the recipients of over $400,000 in funding and were immersed in a selective Y-combinator-type program with other engineers and product builders. My cohort had just two women including myself, which was a shock to me since my field of psychology is majority female. The greater community at large consisted of a typical tech profile, consisting of largely white or South East Asian descent or Indian descent, male gurus. While investors and founders alike were careful enough to pronounce the South East Asian and Indian-American names flawlessly, I flinched when every single person I spoke with mispronounced my first name even though I often corrected them. After receiving a list of the previous fellows in the cohorts before me, I felt strange when I later noticed that I was the first Black woman to be in all cohorts by that point. I had so many questions about why it was the first time a group of people wouldn't pronounce my name right despite my husband, his friends, and myself pronouncing it correctly to others. I pondered these questions as the mispronunciations kept flowing, and felt like I was subtly being put in my place. I wondered if someone or a small group encouraged my mispronounced name to the group in order for me to be reminded of the fact that I didn't belong here, that I was here largely because I happened to be tagged along with my three male co-founders. Of course, I felt silly for that thought, but I had a difficult time rationalizing why my name was consistently mispronounced. I at first forgave the lack of diversity as a result of the community being at the top of the tech-funnel pipeline. I was excited and did my part and referred several Black individuals and minority women whose academic and work profiles were comparable to those in my cohort.

As a neurodivergent Black woman, I certainly felt out of place on the surface, but I noticed class and location differences made my husband and his friends feel uncomfortable as well. Culture shock hit my co-founders hard when the All American cohort confidently discussed their individual accomplishments while my husband and friends were accustomed to showing their completed work rather than upselling their incremental progress like their US counterparts.

Additionally, most products being built were solely profit-focused, such as capitalizing on open source protocols, and selling luxury software to businesses and consumers alike. The highly capitalistic nature of the community made my husband and friends from their communal background scratch their heads.

I remembered how my teenage self, when uncomfortable with people and their ambitions, felt more at peace eating in the bathroom instead of the cafeteria. With my present grown-up self, I felt proud that therapy had helped me gain the clarity that I needed to stop chasing prestige and money, but rather to be happy with the impact I was able to make with the bit I had. It hit me that the involuntary lessons I learned from previous social setbacks and mental health crises somehow made me a few steps ahead of other ambitious individuals who had neither been ill nor challenged outside of their culture. I shed happy tears when I prayed for some of those I spoke with in the community to find their own peace, in a less traumatizing way hopefully.

Unfortunately, our highly anticipated company and fintech software did not ultimately succeed in this environment. After reaching out for some closure, I ceased contact with some remaining members after I was reminded that all still mispronounced my name. I discovered that I had been wearing rose-colored glasses regarding the perceived inclusive culture of the founder community. I later learned that none of the diverse, highly qualified, Black female individuals that I referred were ever contacted. Thankfully, I had dealt with snubbing and isolation in previous years when I was in a worse mental state. The work that I had done on myself, for myself, made this experience significantly less traumatizing. Of course, the ending of this endeavor happened in Kenya, far away from home while on a month-long business trip. My husband and I found ourselves in Nairobi for a few more weeks without a job or immediate future plans. As if the trip wasn't enough of a roller coaster, the two of us celebrated with joy when we found out we were expecting our first child shortly after I wheezed through a safari bike ride. I realized I had no choice but to continue to live out the Hedonic Flywheel Effect concept I coined. As I knew this was an opportune chance to focus on another of my interests alone just as the Hedonic Fly-wheel Effect would want. After the success of my book *Afrotistic*, I decided to take the risk of writing more frequently. It was time to show the world how all people could triumph while being ourselves and looking out for others.

The world is just as harsh as it has always been, and for myself and many of the Black autistic individuals I met in this book project, it is as unfair as it may always be. However, I reflected on people like Jason and Afiniki, who uplifted their hometowns in times of crisis. I remembered Cortez, Olivia, and Akha who utilized their talents to make others who felt bullied and ostracized feel less alone in the world. The true essence of Ujima, I realized, is following in their footsteps toward the future, rather than the bathroom-eating individualistic culture I left in the past. The way to make a better world and community for my future child and others coming behind me was to not complain about the bad, but to get up and showcase the good happening all around.

There's a big task in front of all of us who wish to do the same, and at times it feels like progress is at the pace of a snail. However, it's empowering for all to look at others featured in this book and understand that, just like a tiny snail racing in Okinawa, Japan, all it takes is to start with a single stride. Fortunately for me, the present book was about one-third written when I was in Nairobi. So, with the Kenyan sun beaming down on a November day, and no groupies in sight, I shrugged, rubbed my belly, and finally sat down to finish telling our stories.

Acknowledgments

Thanks to the Black autistic individuals in this book who I've met or reconnected with, and with whom 10 percent of my royalties are being shared. Thanks especially to James: James Mosely from Chapter 2 and I have teamed up to create a decentralized "go-fundme" to fund an additional 10 percent for the organizations we all represent.

James is hyperfocused on the pursuit of knowledge. He's enthusiastic about the future of technology, especially Web3. We have created a fund that will pool together the second 10 percent of my royalty payments plus any additional donations for all of our organizations across the world. Presently, James is the first paid contractor on this project. This fund is a subset of my nonprofit I'm Heard Inc. It will be governed by James, myself, and every autistic individual featured in this book. Presently, it is maintained to fund ourselves and the organizations the autistic features run. Our three researchers featured, Mariajosé Paton, Kiera Adams, and Franckie Castro-Ramirez, have each nominated an additional organization to be in the allocation pool including Autism Women and Nonbinary Network, Neuroclastic, and Autism Self Advocacy Network.

Donations and other forms of encouragement are welcome for the fund. We plan to expand it to be a fundraising and grant allowance source that neurodivergent, disabled, and individuals with mental illnesses could access for capital for themselves and various projects. Unlike traditional centralized funds, our decentralized one would be different in that all those who are a part of the fund can vote to approve or disapprove additional funding allocations. Autistic voices or own voice in question (disabled, racial minorities, individuals with mental illnesses, etc.) who the funding would benefit will also have to have the majority vote for the service funding to be allocated. As the saying goes, there would be "nothing about us, without us" in this fund. If you're interested in donating to the fund, please sign up at this link: www.autistic.black.

References

Abrahams, D. (n.d.) Why designing for accessibility helps everyone. Blog. ai-Media.tv. https://blog.ai-media.tv/blog/why-designing-for-accessibility-helps-everyone.

Adams, K. L., Murphy, J., Catmur, C., & Bird, G. (2022) The role of interoception in the overlap between eating disorders and autism: Methodological considerations. *European Eating Disorders Review*, 30(5), 501–509.

Akha Khumalo (n.d.) *Akha Khumalo: In My Own Words*. https://akhaswords.home.blog.

Allman-Badwin, L. (2014, September 25) A wealth of Black history in Buffalo. *New York Amsterdam News*. https://amsterdamnews.com/news/2014/09/25/wealth-black-history-buffalo.

Anderson, L. M., Lowry, L. S., & Wuensch, K. L. (2015) Racial differences in adolescents' answering questions about suicide. *Death Studies*, 39(10), 60.

Aylward, B. S., Gal-Szabo, D. E., & Taraman, S. (2021) Racial, ethnic, and sociodemographic disparities in diagnosis of children with autism spectrum disorder. *Journal of Developmental and Behavioral Pediatrics*, 42(8), 682.

Bailey, A., Le Couteur, A., Gottesman, I., Bolton, P., *et al.* (1995) Autism as a strongly genetic disorder: Evidence from a British twin study. *Psychological Medicine*, 25(1), 63–77.

Baron-Cohen, S. (2002) The extreme male brain theory of autism. *Trends in Cognitive Sciences*, 6(6), 248–254.

Cassidy, S., Hannant, P., Tavassoli, T., Allison, C., Smith, P., & Baron-Cohen, S. (2016) Dyspraxia and autistic traits in adults with and without autism spectrum conditions. *Molecular Autism*, 7, 1–6.

Castro-Ramirez, F., Al-Suwaidi, M., Garcia, P., Rankin, O., Ricard, J. R., & Nock, M. K. (2021) Racism and poverty are barriers to the treatment of youth mental health concerns. *Journal of Clinical Child & Adolescent Psychology*, 50(4), 534–546.

Centers for Disease Control and Prevention (2018, April 26) *Spotlight On: Racial and Ethnic Differences in Children Identified with Autism Spectrum Disorder (ASD)*. www.cdc.gov/ncbddd/autism/addm-community-report/ differences-in-children.html.

Churchard, A., Ryder, M., Greenhill, A., & Mandy, W. (2019) The prevalence of autistic traits in a homeless population. *Autism*, 23(3), 665–676.

Craft, S. (2018, August 31) Females and Aspergers: A checklist. *The Art of Autism*. https://the-art-of-autism.com/females-and-aspergers-a-checklist.

Dababnah, S., Shaia, W. E., Campion, K., & Nichols, H. M. (2018) "We had to keep pushing": Caregivers' perspectives on autism screening and referral practices of black children in primary care. *Intellectual and Developmental Disabilities*, 56(5), 321–336.

Dattaro, L. (2022, May 27) Spectrum 10K gets green light from ethics agency. *Spectrum | Autism Research News*. www.spectrumnews.org/news/spectrum-10k-gets-green-light-from-ethics-agency.

Eckerd M. (2021, August) Are we giving autistic children PTSD from school? *Psychology Today*. www.psychologytoday.com/gb/blog/everyday-neurodiversity/202108/are-we-giving-autistic-children-ptsd-school.

Franke, K. B., Paton, M., & Weist, M. (2020) Building policy support for school mental health in South Carolina. *School Psychology Review*, 50(1), 110–121.

Gardener, H., Spiegelman, D., & Buka, S. L. (2009) Prenatal risk factors for autism: Comprehensive meta-analysis. *The British Journal of Psychiatry*, 195(1), 7–14.

Gross, L. (2009) A broken trust: Lessons from the vaccine–autism wars: Researchers long ago rejected the theory that vaccines cause autism, yet many parents don't believe them. Can scientists bridge the gap between evidence and doubt? *PLoS Biology*, 7(5), e1000114.

Harvard School of Public Health (2020) Black people more than three times as likely as white people to be killed during a police encounter. *Harvard School of Public Health News.* https://www.hsph.harvard.edu/news/hsph-in-the-news/blacks-whites-police-deaths-disparity

Hall, R. (2022) *Wake: The Hidden History of Women-Led Slave Revolts.* New York: Simon and Schuster.

Hoek, H. W. & Van Hoeken, D. (2003) Review of the prevalence and incidence of eating disorders. *International Journal of Eating Disorders,* 34(4), 383–396.

Hollocks, M. J., Lerh, J. W., Magiati, I., Meiser-Stedman, R., & Brugha, T. S. (2019) Anxiety and depression in adults with autism spectrum disorder: A systematic review and meta-analysis. *Psychological Medicine,* 49(4), 559–572.

Horowitz, J. (2022, July 25) Francis begs forgiveness for "evil" Christians inflicted on indigenous people. *The New York Times.* www.nytimes.com/live/2022/07/25/world/pope-francis-canada-visit.

Hu, Y., Pereira, A. M., Gao, X., Campos, B. M., *et al.* (2021) Right temporoparietal junction underlies avoidance of moral transgression in autism spectrum disorder. *Journal of Neuroscience,* 41(8), 1699–1715.

I-ASC (n.d.) *Spelling to Communicate | S2C.* https://i-asc.org.

Jones, L., Goddard, L., Hill, E. L., Henry, L. A., & Crane, L. (2014) Experiences of receiving a diagnosis of autism spectrum disorder: A survey of adults in the United Kingdom. *Journal of Autism and Developmental Disorders,* 44(12), 3033–3044.

Kilpatrick, A. (2022, June 4) A 911 dispatcher has been fired over mishandling a Buffalo shooting call. NPR. www.npr.org/2022/05/20/1100497516/a-911-dispatcher-may-be-fired-for-allegedly-mishandling-a-buffalo-shooting-call.

Kinouani, G. (2020) Silencing, power and racial trauma in groups. *Group Analysis,* 53(2), 145–161.

Klauck, S. M. (2006) Genetics of autism spectrum disorder. European Journal of Human Genetics, 14(6), 714–720.

Kowalski, D. R. (1972) The Ku Klux Klan in Buffalo, New York, 1922–1924: A case study. Doctoral dissertation, University of North Carolina at Greensboro.

Ledur, J., Rabinowitz, K., & Galocha, A. (2022, June 2) There have been over

200 mass shootings so far in 2022. *Washington Post.* www.washingtonpost. com/nation/2022/06/02/mass-shootings-in-2022.

Medearis, A. S. (1994) *The Seven Days of Kwanzaa.* New York: Scholastic Inc.

Morris, D. (2019) Shaka, Zulu chief. *Encyclopædia Britannica.* www.britannica. com/biography/Shaka-Zulu-chief.

National Alliance to End Homelessness (2020, October) *Racial Inequality— National Alliance to End Homelessness.* National Alliance to End Homelessness. https://endhomelessness.org/homelessness-in-america/what-causes-homelessness/inequality.

National Science Foundation (2019) *Doctorate Recipients from U.S. Universities: 2019.* National Center for Science and Engineering Statistics, Alexandria, VA, 21–308. https://ncses.nsf.gov/pubs/nsf21308.

NBC News (May, 2022) 1 dead, 5 injured, man arrested in shooting at California Asian church reception. *NBC News.* www.nbcnews.com/news/us-news/ multiple-victims-reported-person-detained-california-church-shooting-rcna28937.

Newschaffer, C. J., Fallin, D., & Lee, N. L. (2002) Heritable and nonheritable risk factors for autism spectrum disorders. *Epidemiologic Reviews, 24*(2), 137–153.

Neurodiversity Hub (n.d.) *Resources for Students, Employers & More.* www. neurodiversityhub.org.

New Living Translation Bible (2021) Carol Stream, IL: Tyndale House Publishers. (Original work published 1996).

NHS (2022) *Autism Statistics, July 2021 to June 2022.* https://digital.nhs.uk/ data-and-information/publications/statistical/autism-statistics/july-2021-to-june-2022.

Nock, M. K., Ramirez, F., & Rankin, O. (2019) Advancing our understanding of the who, when, and why of suicide risk. *JAMA Psychiatry, 76*(1), 11–12.

Ogunyemi, I. (2022, May 25) Nigeria has fewer than 300 psychiatrists for its over 200 million population—Obindo, APN president. *Tribune Online.* https://tribuneonlineng.com/nigeria-has-fewer-than-300-psychiatrists-for-its-over-200-million-population-obindo-apn-president.

Omeiza, K. A. (2018, November 25) Beauty and the Beans *Kala's Detour.* kalaomeiza.com/blog

Omeiza, K. A. (2021) Why neurodiversity inclusion at universities benefits everyone. *The Mighty*. https://themighty.com/topic/autism-spectrum-disorder/autism-neurodiversity-inclusion-universities.

Pardung, K. P. K. & Chukwuemeka, G. S. (2023) The history of religion in Nigeria. *Dynamic Journal of Humanities, Social and Management Sciences*. Richmond, IN. https://scholar.google.com/citations?view_op=view_citation&hl=en&user=-UIILCoAAAAJ&citation_for_view=-UIILCoAAAAJ:mvPsJ3kp5DgC.

Price, M., Weisz, J., McKetta, S., Hollinsaid, N. L., *et al.* (2020) Are psychotherapies less effective for black youth in communities with higher levels of anti-black racism? Doi.org/10.17605/OSF.IO/UG3FX.

reliefweb (2017) The power of speech: A Translators without Borders project highlighting language barriers for internally displaced people (IDPs) in northeast Nigeria. https://reliefweb.int/report/nigeria/power-speech-translators-without-borders-project-highlighting-language-barriers.

Santangelo, S. L. & Tsatsanis, K. (2005) What is known about autism: Genes, brain, and behavior. *American Journal of Pharmacogenomics*, 5, 71–92.

Sedgewick, F., Hill, V., & Pellicano, E. (2018) Parent perspectives on autistic girls' friendships and futures. *Autism & Developmental Language Impairments*, 3. Doi 2396941518794497.

South Africa (n.d.) *African Tribes*. www.thesouthafricaguide.com/african-tribes/african-tribes-south-african-tribes-south-africa-culture.

Werling, D. M. & Geschwind, D. H. (2013) Sex differences in autism spectrum disorders. *Current Opinion in Neurology*, 26(2), 146.

Whitlock, A., Fulton, K., Lai, M. C., Pellicano, E., & Mandy, W. (2020) Recognition of girls on the autism spectrum by primary school educators: An experimental study. *Autism Research*, 13(8), 1358–1372.